ACADEMIC LIBRARIANSHIP IN THE 21ST CENTURY

ACADEMIC LIBRARIANSHIP IN THE 21ST CENTURY

CLAUDIA M. GARCIA
AND
TERESA A. FLORES
EDITORS

Nova Science Publishers, Inc.
New York

For permission to use material from this book please contact us:
Telephone 631-231-7269; Fax 631-231-8175
Web Site: http://www.novapublishers.com

LIBRARY OF CONGRESS CATALOGING-IN-PUBLICATION DATA

Academic librarianship in the 21st century / [edited by] Claudia M. Garcia and Teresa A. Flores.

p. cm.

Includes bibliographical references and index.

ISBN 978-1-60456-865-3

1. Academic libraries. 2. Library copyright policies--United States. 3. Fair use (Copyright)--United States. 4. Bibliography--Methodology. I. Garcia, Claudia M. II. Flores, Teresa A.

Z675.U5A315 2009 027.7--dc22 2009006347

Published by Nova Science Publishers, Inc. ✣ New York

CONTENTS

PREFACE

This book explores some of the roles and challenges that academic libraries face in the 21st century. Developments in certain software programs are examined, particularly as they enable library patrons to access, download, retrieve and import bibliographic records from the databases of academic universities and manage their bibliographies more efficiently and conveniently. The important roles of academic libraries in promoting the use of such bibliographic management software by providing needed facilities and organizing training courses for faculties, students and researchers are also discussed. Furthermore, today's academic libraries are often forced to enter into a significant number of licensing agreements every year for access to electronic resources. As a result, libraries may find themselves unable to provide the level of intended access to electronic resources in accordance with their goals or mission statement. This book discusses how libraries may become more cognizant of the implications that license agreements have to limit their ability to provide access to their patrons. An overview of current trends, legislation, and litigation related to fair use of intellectual property is also provided as it impacts academic libraries in the United States. Recent developments in fair use issues are explored as well, such as scholarly publishing and library electronic reserves, and examples of initiatives currently being used on campuses to retain, secure, and exercise fair use rights in the twenty-first century are given. Finally, Library of Congress subject headings (LCSH) have been a very important component of bibliographic records for many years. The use of tightly controlled vocabulary to create specific subject headings provides greater precision in subject searches to help direct patrons to the most relevant materials. The authors of this book provide feasible suggestions for future improvements in assignment and usage of LCSH to make them easier to use, understand, and apply.

Chapter 1 - Today's academic libraries are forced to enter into a significant number of licensing agreements every year for access to electronic resources. Vendors, or licensors, have the power to dictate the terms and conditions set forth in the license agreement. While libraries may attempt to negotiate and change certain terms, their attempts are often futile or met with strong resistance. Ultimately, the terms of these license agreements dictate the ability of libraries to provide access to electronic resources for their patrons. The license terms may limit or curtail access by certain patron groups, including alumni, walk-in users, the public, and other higher education institutions. The license agreement may also eliminate or restrict libraries' abilities to rely on the fair use provisions or engage in interlibrary loan under copyright law. Additionally, libraries may choose to or be forced for economic reasons to discontinue their print collection of titles that are also available electronically. These libraries may be left scrambling to provide access to these same resources if the licensor eliminates or changes its titles, years of coverage, or ceases to exist as an entity. As a result of these scenarios, libraries may find themselves unable to provide the level of intended access to electronic resources in accordance with their goals or mission statement. This inability to provide access can be directly tied back to the license agreement and its terms and conditions.

Chapter 2 - Google Scholar, Amazon.com, Wikiepedia, Flicker, MySpace, social networking, open access, and easy retrieval of electronic resources and services create higher user expectations for an academic library's collections and services. In this competitive environment of content providers and users' growing expectations, academic libraries face a difficult task in providing the most satisfying ways of delivering information and services to their patrons. To what extent should academic libraries recognize the users' information needs in the areas of service and collections? Is it possible for libraries to fulfill users' growing expectations toward libraries' collections and services? What would happen if Google failed?

In searching for answers to these questions this article not only presents the LibQUAL +TM survey results that helped to determine users' satisfaction and expectations of the quality of library service, but it also evaluates the outcomes of the survey that were implemented to improve the quality of offered library services. Assessment of service quality standards by library users is becoming a crucial element in future advances taking place in academic libraries. These advances will not only influence the quality of offered services but also determine the new formats of services. They will create demand for new organizational and spatial libraries' structure, cooperation, and integrated services, which will better fulfill educational and research university missions.

For more than 2000 years people have considered libraries as treasures of knowledge, information, and cultures. Their educational and cultural values rested in the contents of library collections. Nevertheless, in this day of prime digital information formats and communication technologies libraries are constantly losing their collection content, which is being intercepted by commercial stockholders such as Google Book Project, Google Scholar, Amazon.com Look Inside, and Microsoft's Windows Live Book Search. Fast development of open access publishing models has provided free and wide access to scholarly resources that were entirely inaccessible to all users years ago. Additionally, Web 2.0 has contributed to easy distribution and exchange of content in forms of text, images, and multimedia through the growing fast social-networking environment of blogs, podcasts, Wikis, MySpace, Facebook, YouTube, and Flicker.

Chapter 3 - This paper is based on a research, Use of the EndNote program for bibliographic management in Srinakharinwirot University's style manual. It describes the situation in Thailand in which bibliographic management software such as EndNote is rarely known and used as a research tool in the academic setting. This situation is caused by the limitation of EndNote as it cannot support Thai language, and is partly caused by the fact that most Thai universities established their own style manuals. The paper reports a study being carried out to solve the problem. In this study, templates for Srinakharinwirot University (SWU) style manual were constructed for creating bibliographies by using EndNote program. Z39.50 connection files for Thai academic libraries were created and tested. This development enables library patrons to access, download, retrieve and import bibliographic records from the databases of academic universities and manage their bibliographies more efficiently and conveniently. Lastly, the author emphasizes the important roles of academic libraries in Thailand in promoting the use of bibliographic management software by providing needed facilities and organizing training courses for faculties, students and researchers.

Chapter 4 - In recent years, the Fair Use doctrine of United States copyright law has been continually tested in the courts. Recently a Judge Alex Kozinski of the 9th U.S. Circuit Court of Appeals went so far as to call fair use a "red herring" and declared that "we should just dump it" (Kozinski & Newman, 1999).

Librarians have been championing the fair use rights of the American public since long before those rights were actually codified by copyright law. However, more recently many librarians and other educators have been hesitant to use certain materials in an educational setting, fearful of attracting the notice of litigious publishers, recording companies, and other content owners. Campuses' legal representation have only increased this feeling of malaise, taking a "better safe than sorry" stance on fair use of intellectual property.

It is difficult to predict the effect that proposed legislation such as the “Intellectual Property Rights Enforcement Act” or the “Curb Illegal Downloading on College Campuses Act of 2007” may have on campuses and libraries; future court cases will also have a large impact on fair use rights as they have been historically exercised. It can be surmised that the cautionary atmosphere already created by the Digital Millennium Copyright Act and other recent legislation will only increase, creating an even more inhibitive environment with regard to educational use of intellectual property.

This chapter will provide an overview of current trends, legislation, and litigation related to fair use of intellectual property as it impacts academic libraries in the United States. It will explore recent developments in fair use issues such as scholarly publishing and library electronic reserves, and give examples of initiatives currently being used on campuses to retain, secure, and exercise fair use rights in the twenty-first century.

Chapter 5 - Library of Congress subject headings (LCSH) have been a very important component of bibliographic records for many years. The use of tightly controlled vocabulary to create specific subject headings provides greater precision in subject searches to help direct patrons to the most relevant materials. Yet subject searches are still the most difficult and problematic search for many patrons who do not understand LCSH structure and have difficulty identifying the exact keywords necessary to complete a comprehensive search.

Cataloging librarians evaluate and identify areas where bibliographic records can be enhanced to provide patrons with as many access points as possible. Ideally, the cataloger evaluates items and then assigns specific subject headings and broader, less-specific subject headings that can be narrowed in scope through the addition of subdivisions. This process increases accessibility to materials by offering more ways to locate them. These subject searches will not provide patrons with a comprehensive list of every item available to them unless these broader subject headings are assigned consistently to materials. Ensuring consistency in subject headings can be difficult because many items are processed through vendor records, shared cataloging databases and localized copy-cataloging practices. While these methods speed up the processing of materials, they do not provide a step where additional subject access points can be consistently added.

A study of subject searches entered by patrons at the University of Oklahoma Libraries over the course of two semesters should allow identification of problematic areas and provide insight into search patterns among the types of subject headings used most. This analysis should also illustrate discrepancies between the keywords used by patrons and the corresponding LCSH for failed subject searches.

The authors hope to provide feasible suggestions for future improvements in assignment and usage of LCSH to make them easier to use, understand, and apply. Eventual goals of this study include: (1) incorporating less-controlled vocabulary that is more user-friendly through broader usage of cross-references; (2) updating and adding new LCSH more quickly to reflect advancements in technology, evolving research and study disciplines, and current events and nomenclature; and (3) developing consistency checks to allow enhancement of bibliographic records to provide more accessibility to materials through subject searches.

Chapter 6 - An overview of the open access literature in Library and Information Science (LIS) is offered. A list of 78 scholarly journals in LIS that are freely available electronically was compiled through the Directory of Open Access Journals (DOAJ). Characteristics of the journals—language, publisher, start year and frequency—were analysed. For each journal its coverage by three major abstracting and indexing services in the field— Library and Information Science Abstracts (LISA), Library, Information Science & Technology Abstracts (LISTA) and Library Literature and Information Science Full Text (LibLit)—was determined. Additionally a list of 48 open access digital repositories in LIS was obtained from the Directory of Open Access Repositories (OpenDOAR). Features of the repositories—language, software, size and contents—were analysed.

In: Academic Librarianship in the 21st Century ISBN: 978-1-60456-865-3
Editors: C. M.Garcia and T. A.Flores ©2009 Nova Science Publishers, Inc.

Chapter 1

THE IMPACT OF LICENSE AGREEMENTS ON ACCESS TO INFORMATION: A CHALLENGE FOR ACADEMIC LIBRARIES

Stacey L. Bowers
Access Services Librarian,University of Denver Sturm College of Law
Westminster Law Library, Denver, Colorado, USA

ABSTRACT

Today's academic libraries are forced to enter into a significant number of licensing agreements every year for access to electronic resources. Vendors, or licensors, have the power to dictate the terms and conditions set forth in the license agreement. While libraries may attempt to negotiate and change certain terms, their attempts are often futile or met with strong resistance. Ultimately, the terms of these license agreements dictate the ability of libraries to provide access to electronic resources for their patrons. The license terms may limit or curtail access by certain patron groups, including alumni, walk-in users, the public, and other higher education institutions. The license agreement may also eliminate or restrict libraries' abilities to rely on the fair use provisions or engage in interlibrary loan under copyright law. Additionally, libraries may choose to or be forced for economic reasons to discontinue their print collection of titles that are also available electronically. These libraries may be left scrambling to provide access to these same resources if the licensor eliminates or changes its titles, years of coverage, or ceases to exist as an entity. As a result of these scenarios, libraries may find themselves unable to provide the level of intended access to electronic resources in accordance with their goals or mission statement. This inability to provide access can be directly tied back to the license agreement and its terms and conditions.

INTRODUCTION

Access is the right of a patron to enter a library and use its collections and resources openly and freely, including the right to use computer systems and online resources (Reitz, 2004). A core value of the American Library Association (ALA) is the concept of access to information. The ALA states, "All information resources that are provided directly or indirectly by the library, regardless of technology, format, or methods of delivery, should be readily, equally, and equitably accessible to all library users" (American Library Association Core Values of Librarianship, 2007). The ALA believes libraries should consider their goals, missions, and objectives, as well as the needs of their communities in determining the best way to provide access to electronic information (American Library Association Access to Electronic Information, Services, and Networks: An Interpretation of the Library Bill of Rights, 2007). Access to electronic information is a critical component of providing and making available resources to a library's patrons. Without access to electronic information, a patron is limited and hindered in his or her ability to engage in effective information retrieval.

An overriding commitment of academic libraries is to provide patrons with access to resources, whether print, electronic, or other formats. These patrons represent a diverse group of individuals, including the primary constituency generally comprised of the institution's students, faculty, and staff. Libraries may also view alumni and other higher education institutions as patrons. In addition, academic libraries at public institutions often serve the general public, a group that consists of a broad array of people ranging from an independent academic researcher to a local community member.

The mission statements of many academic libraries at both private and public institutions state that one of their goals is to provide patrons with access to information resources and services. While mission statements vary, the following represent a mix of various libraries' missions. A private academic law library states that its mission is to provide its students, faculty, and alumni, as well as members of the legal bar community and the public, "... with access to the broadest array of legal information sources" (Westminster Law Library Mission Statement, 2007). A public university's law library states, "The primary mission...is to evaluate, select, organize and provide access to information resources and services that support the instructional, research, and service programs of the students, faculty, and staff..." (University of Colorado Law Library Collection Development Policy, 2007). In addition to serving the needs of the greater university community, this law library also serves other groups, including the state's legal community, other academic institutions, and the general public (University of Colorado Law Library).

An academic library located on a campus serving three diverse public institutions, "...aspires to provide the best of both traditional and electronic information resources and services" (Mission of the Auraria Library, 2007). In addition to serving the patrons of the three institutions on the campus, the library also serves any resident of the state (Mission of the Auraria Library). A public university's academic library has a goal of sharing its resources with other higher education institutions, both nationally and internationally (University of Colorado at Boulder University Libraries Mission Statement, 2007). A private university library states that, "The library links information and the university community regardless of the location of the information or the individual seeking it" (University of Denver Penrose Library Frequently Asked Questions, 2007). Another private university library sets as one of its goals the provision of access to materials that are located both within and outside the library for its university community (Regis University Libraries Mission Statement, 2007). In addition, this library engages in community outreach by offering access to government publications and local area materials to the general public (Regis University Libraries Mission Statement).

What is readily apparent from this mix of mission statements is that academic libraries, whether serving a private or public institution, establish broad goals regarding access to information. While the primary goal remains serving the institution's main constituency of students, faculty, and staff, these libraries also believe in providing access to alumni, other academic institutions, and the public. In addition, academic libraries often view it as crucial to provide access both on-site at the library, and remotely regardless of where the patron is currently located.

While libraries can provide wide-ranging access to print materials, whether to their primary patrons, alumni, other institutions, or the public, these same libraries may not be able to meet this goal as it pertains to electronic materials. The ability to provide a broad range of access to electronic resources is often curtailed by outside factors. These hindrances include specific language in the license agreement limiting or denying the use of these electronic resources by certain patrons and/or eliminating the library's right to provide information from these resources through interlibrary loan, and economic constraints due to the cost of licensing fees. In addition, as libraries spend a larger percentage of their budgets on electronic resources, they may no longer collect those same resources in print format. As a result, the goal of providing broad-based access is curtailed.

Shift From Paper to Electronic Resources

With the advent and growth of materials that are available electronically, there has been a shift by libraries toward providing more and more access to resources only in electronic format. In particular, many libraries are cancelling subscriptions to their print journal collections when they are able to make the journals available to patrons through an electronic database option. This shift from paper to both paper and electronic, or to electronic only has occurred for a variety of reasons.

Many libraries have determined they cannot afford to maintain both the print and electronic versions of the same resource. As a result, libraries often determine which version to provide for patrons, and more frequently than not the electronic version is selected. For some libraries, it is a clear cost advantage to shift from paper to electronic resources. Many libraries license the content from electronic database vendors as a consortium. As a result of these consolidated purchases, libraries may be able to provide electronic access for less than the cost of print access (Roether & Koepf, 2005).

In addition to economic considerations, libraries may take into account space issues when making a determination as to whether or not to maintain print resources that are also available electronically. Available space and shelves are often at a premium in academic libraries. One way to solve the problem of limited shelf space is to move print copies of journals that are available electronically to off-site storage and also to discontinue the collection of print journals available through the library's electronic databases (Wallenius, 2007).

Another consideration that libraries may take into account when determining whether or not to retain the print version of a resource that is also available electronically is the level of recorded use (Roether & Koepf, 2005). Libraries may determine that the extra cost and usage of space to maintain print versions of those journals most frequently used by students and faculty in their research is a prudent investment, even when it's more costly to subscribe to the print version rather than the electronic version (Roether & Koepf, 2005).

The shift from print to electronic resources brings both advantages and disadvantages. By moving to electronic resources, libraries can often provide a more in-depth collection of journal titles for patrons than they could in a print only format (Wallenius, 2007). Electronic resources generally allow libraries to provide broader access to its authorized users both on-site and off-site because remote access is available around the clock from any location. Another advantage of access through electronic resources is the constant availability to multiple patrons at the same time (Wallenius). In addition, electronic materials do not inhabit physical space in the library, which may allow libraries to add additional print titles to the collection that they did not previously have the space to accommodate. By shifting to more electronic resources, libraries can also meet the demands of many of their patrons for instant access, anytime and from anyplace.

Despite these advantages, there are also a number of disadvantages in the shift from paper to electronic materials. One disadvantage is the cost of licensing access to electronic resources. For many libraries providing electronic databases to its patrons may be cost prohibitive. Another significant disadvantage is that libraries have little or no control over the database provider because they do not own the content; libraries only license or lease access to these resources. The vendor chooses which content to keep, add, or delete from its database. Many licensing agreements allow the vendor to change the titles and years of coverage contained in its database offerings at its sole discretion. As a result of the vendor's ability to change its offerings on a whim, a journal title that is available during one subscription period may not be available during the next period. In the event that libraries have cancelled a print title in favor of electronic only access, they may find themselves with no copies of that particular title if the database vendor chooses to remove it from their list of available offerings. As a result, access to that particular resource is completely eliminated, both electronically and in print.

Another problem with electronic databases is the potential delay in publication of the content. There can be a significant time delay from publication of the print version to availability of the electronic version, depending upon the particular database vendor and title. In some instances, the electronic version may not be available for up to six months after publication of the print resource (Roether & Koepf, 2007). In those cases where the library only provides access through the electronic version, patrons are forced to wait for access to current information or must find an alternative means of access.

Relevant Copyright Provisions

In order to fully understand its rights and how best to negotiate the license agreement, the library must have a clear understanding of various copyright law provisions and how these provisions influence its ability to provide access for patrons. In particular, the library must understand the impact of licensing arrangements in regard to Section 109 of copyright law, the first sale doctrine. The library must also pay close attention to those license agreement provisions which impact its ability to rely on Sections 107 and 108 of copyright law, fair use and interlibrary loan. While the original intent of copyright law was to "balance the access rights of the public with the profit and control interests of copyright holders," license agreements have shifted that balance (Bartow, 2001, p. 833). It is now the copyright holder who maintains the power and in regard to electronic resources, that party is the database vendor. In today's reality, the license agreement terms override existing copyright law and the library is bound by the provisions of the license in regard to what it can and cannot do with an electronic resource (Johnson, 2004).

The library's rights under the doctrine of first sale are completely eliminated by the license agreement structure. Under copyright law this doctrine permits a library to purchase material and subsequently loan, resell, or gift that material to patrons (U.S. Copyright Act §109). However, when a library enters into a license agreement, it is not purchasing the electronic content; it is only licensing or leasing that material. As a result, the library has not engaged in an actual and outright purchase, and so the rights provided under the first sale doctrine do not apply to the electronic resource. In essence, this means the library cannot loan the material, resell the material, or give the material away as it can with print materials that it purchases outright. As a result, the license agreement structure curtails the library's rights under copyright law and its ability to provide broad access to the electronic resource. The consequence of losing the right of first sale under license agreements is that the library must comply with the license agreement terms, which means strictly controlling when and where access can be made available to patrons. The library cannot loan, resell, or gift any of the electronic content unless permitted under the license agreement, which is highly unlikely.

The fair use provisions of copyright law are essential to the library and its ability to provide access to patrons. Fair use allows the library, as well as its patrons, to make use of copyrighted material for purposes such as criticism, comment, news reporting, teaching, scholarship, or research (U.S. Copyright Act §107). Pursuant to the fair use doctrine, a library or its patrons can make copies of copyrighted material provided it falls within fair use. In making a determination of whether or not the library is engaging in fair use, the library must consider the following four factors: (i) the purpose and character of the use; (ii) the nature of the work; (iii) the amount used in proportion to the whole; and, (iv) the effect of the use on the potential market and value of the work (U.S. Copyright Act §107). As a result of the fair use provision, a library is often able to make photocopies of copyrighted works for their patrons when the patrons are using such materials for teaching, scholarship, or research. Without fair use rights, a library would be greatly hindered in its ability to serve and assist students and faculty in their studies and research. For example, if the license agreement contains a provision which eliminates the right of fair use, a faculty member would not be permitted to make multiple copies of the electronic content for his or her students for teaching purposes. A patron would be unable to make a copy of information contained in the electronic database for research or scholarship purposes. While some license agreements specifically eliminate fair use rights, it is even more typical for a license agreement to restrict or eliminate the library's right to engage in interlibrary loan transactions.

Section 108 of copyright law allows libraries to engage in the practice of interlibrary loan. This provision allows a library to make a copy of a work and distribute that copy to a user who has requested the work either from that library or through another library (U.S. Copyright Act §108(d)). The copy must become the property of the user who requested it, and the library must believe that the user will use the copy only for the purposes of private study, scholarship, or research (U.S. Copyright Act §108(d)). Furthermore, the library must prominently display appropriate copyright warning language where interlibrary loan orders are accepted and on the related order forms (U.S. Copyright Act §108(d)).

If the library enters into a license agreement which preempts its rights under the interlibrary loan provision of copyright law, the library will have a difficult time providing access to some of its patrons. The library will be prevented from printing a copy of any electronic content contained in that database and loaning it pursuant to Section 108. While the library may have retained its fair use rights, which would allow for a copy to be made in certain situations, the lack of rights to engage in interlibrary loan preempts the ability of anyone who is not an authorized user under the license agreement to access the electronic content. As a result, "the tradition of libraries freely lending, borrowing, and exchanging portions of their collections with other libraries" is restricted or eliminated (Bartow, 2001, p. 826). When the library is not able to engage in interlibrary loan transactions as a result of the license agreement, many of its potential patrons endure a great disservice -- severely limited access. This license restriction results in the curtailment of one of the foundations of libraries, interlibrary loan.

When a library enters into any license agreement, the first right that is stripped is its ability to rely on the doctrine of first sale. In addition, many license agreements also restrict or eliminate the library's ability to rely on Sections 107 and 108 of the copyright law. As a result, the library gives up control to provide the services needed and often demanded by its patrons. This loss can deter the library from its stated mission of providing access to information. Once the library has entered into the license agreement, it cannot rely on copyright law because it provides broader rights. The library must abide by the language of the license agreement, no matter how severely such language restricts the library in its ability to engage in fair use and interlibrary loan transactions, and ultimately provide the access it has promised.

LICENSE AGREEMENTS

A direct consequence of this continuing shift from paper to electronic resources is the licensing agreement. The license agreement is simply the contract entered into between the licensee, (i.e., the library), and the licensor, the vendor providing the electronic database and access to its content. Electronic databases are comprehensive collections of digitized information generally related to a specific area or field of study and are designed for ease of access (Reitz, 2004). The database vendor typically leases or purchases the electronic content and makes it available using their specific search software or interface (Reitz). Vendors protect their rights to the electronic product by requiring libraries to enter into the license agreement in order to gain access to the content. In most cases, the vendor drafts and provides the license agreement to the licensee. In some instances the licensee may be able to negotiate various provisions of the agreement, and in other cases the license may not be subject to negotiation.

Like most legally binding contracts, the license agreement contains numerous terms and provisions that govern the contractual relationship between the parties. A number of these provisions impact a library's ability to provide its patrons with access to this electronic information. The specific provisions that are most likely to impact who the library can provide access to and how such access can be provided include: (i) the definition of authorized user; (ii) the definition of authorized site; (iii) the scope of permitted uses; and, (iv) whether or not the library has kept its fair use and interlibrary loan rights pursuant to copyright law. Additionally, the provision addressing whether or not the library has the right to create an archival data file may determine the library's ability to provide on-going access to the electronic information.

The definition of authorized user is critical in every licensing situation and determines who is legally permitted to use the electronic database. The library must have a clear understanding of its patrons and should seek to define the term authorized users based on this knowledge. The library should also take into account its stated goals and mission when determining who should be included as authorized users. In most license agreements, the term authorized user includes students, faculty, and staff affiliated with the academic institution, and walk-in patrons as permitted by the library. In some situations, the license agreement may attempt to limit authorized users to students, faculty, and staff affiliated with a particular unit of the institution, such as a law school or business school. In many instances, the standard definition of authorized user does not meet the needs, goals, or mission of the library, or the expectations of its patrons. The library may be committed to providing broader access and want to include visiting faculty, adjunct faculty, alumni, the public, or other groups, but may be unable to do so as a result of the limited definition of authorized user pursuant to the license agreement.

The inclusion of walk-in patrons in the definition of authorized users generally allows the library to offer access to visiting or adjunct faculty, alumni, or the public. However, if the license agreement stipulates walk-in users at the library versus at the institution as a whole, the library would only be permitted to offer access to those persons actually present in the library and using a computer in the facility. As a result, the license prevents the visiting or adjunct faculty from accessing the resource from their office computer or from anywhere other than the library.

More often than not, alumni are not specifically listed in the definition of authorized user. This means access can only be provided to this group of patrons in a limited manner, if at all. If the license agreement allows for walk-in users, then alumni who live locally could walk into the library and utilize the electronic resource on-site. However, many alumni do not remain in the area after graduation and although the library may have a mission of providing access to them, it will not be able to meet that goal because they cannot utilize the electronic resource from any location other than on-site. In those limited instances where the license agreement does specifically allow for access to alumni, it may still be difficult to make such access available to that user group remotely. It is often cost prohibitive to even consider including alumni in the group of authorized users. The vendor may charge a premium for allowing this type of broad-based patron access to persons who are not currently affiliated with the institution.

Unlike the print resource, which any library patron who is permitted to use the library may access and utilize, the electronic resource is restricted to only those authorized users as defined in the license agreement (Roether & Koepf, 2005). As a result, the library should attempt to define authorized user as broadly as possible so that it can meet the overriding goal of providing access to all its patrons. However, the definition of authorized user often conflicts with or limits the library's stated goals or mission. As a result, resources that were once readily accessible to any patron of the library now reside behind the wall of a proprietary database that is accessible by far fewer patrons (Wand, 2005). With access provided electronically in lieu of print, these resources may be forever lost to those patrons who do not fall within the authorized user definition.

Another concern for the library is the omission from the definition of authorized users of a group of particular patrons, such as staff, visiting faculty, or walk-in users. In that case, the library may find itself in the precarious situation of not being able to offer the electronic resource to them or having to attempt to renegotiate that portion of the license agreement. The library should never assume that unlisted patron groups are covered in the definition of authorized users. No matter the end result, the library must abide by the definition of authorized user and ultimately, it is this definition that will determine who can and cannot access the electronic information.

In conjunction with authorized user is the concept of authorized site. This license agreement provision determines the location from which users may access the electronic database — on-site only, or on-site and remotely. If the library desires to make the electronic content available to its authorized users remotely, the license must specifically state that remote access is permitted (Harris, 2002). While most license agreements allow the library's primary patrons, students, faculty, and staff, to access the electronic resource off-site, the license does not often allow other library users, alumni and the public, to do so. As a result, alumni and public patrons will be relegated to using the electronic database on-site at the library. While the library may state that it provides access to alumni and the public, these site restrictions will limit access to only those persons who have the ability to visit the library. While many license agreements allow on-site and remote access for the library's primary patrons, this is not always the case. In some instances, the library will have to negotiate the right to provide off-site access to the electronic database even for students, faculty, and staff. This may result in additional licensing fees. Due to these added costs, the library may be reluctant or unable to provide any off-site access, even to its primary patrons.

Libraries must also pay careful attention to the license agreement and the permitted uses it stipulates for the electronic resource. In some instances, the database vendor through the license agreement will limit use of the electronic resource to academic research or educational use only (Lowry, 1993). In that case, patrons of the library may only utilize the electronic resource when they are engaged in academically based research or educational purposes. This means that even the library's primary patrons cannot use the resource for work-related research, an internship experience, or for pleasure. Additionally, if the license only allows for academic research usage or educational use, alumni, walk-in users, and the public would be prohibited from utilizing that resource unless engaged in some type of academic or educational research. As a result of this type of license agreement provision, the library is required to police patrons who have access to the electronic information and the manner in which they use the resource (Bartow, 2001). Additionally, limitations on permitted uses impact the librarians and their ability to utilize the electronic resource to assist patrons. This situation will require the librarians to determine if the patron is engaged in a permitted use and to determine whether or not they can utilize that particular electronic resource to assist the patron. License agreement provisions that limit permitted uses of the electronic resource are very difficult to govern. They require more stringent standards regarding access to ensure that those persons engaged in use of the resource are allowed to do so. Otherwise, the library may find itself in violation of the license agreement.

Another concern with any license agreement is its structure as a license (or lease) and not an outright purchase. By characterizing the transaction as a license, the database vendor is preventing the library from engaging in a purchase; therefore, the library cannot simply do what it desires in compliance with copyright law with the electronic resource in the ways that are possible with a print resource. As a result, license agreements compromise library patrons' access to information in a way that is not possible with books or paper journals (Bartow, 2001).

In addition to eliminating first sale rights, many license agreements restrict or override a library's ability to engage in fair use of the electronic content or engage in interlibrary loans of such content. While these rights are granted under copyright law, the license agreement can contract away those rights from the library. Some license agreements restrict or eliminate entirely the library's right to engage in interlibrary loan transactions. The license may stipulate that the library can only engage in interlibrary loan within the institution or only if the library also owns a print version of the electronic material. In other cases, the license may explicitly prohibit all interlibrary loan transactions no matter the reason — academic use or otherwise. The library must carefully review any license agreement provision that affects copyright law and attempts to restrict or eliminate those rights. The library must then make a conscious determination as to whether or not those license agreement infringements are acceptable to the library and its goals and mission.

A final concern is whether or not the library has been granted the right to archive an electronic copy of the database and its content. Unlike previous electronic products, such as CD-ROMs and disks, when the electronic content is stored and only available through remote Internet access, the library no longer holds or owns a tangible product (Klinefelter, 2001). Since the library has no control over the electronic resource, it has no ability to preserve that information (Klinefelter). While some licenses permit the library to make an archival copy of the electronic content, in many cases the database vendor retains all archival rights (Klinefelter). If the library is not permitted to store an archival copy of the electronic content, it may find itself without access to any of that information, particularly in the event where the vendor chooses to delete specific titles or years of coverage from its database collection or ceases to exist as a corporate entity. As a result, the library can no longer provide access to any of its patrons, even if they meet the definition of authorized user.

IMPACTS AND CONSEQUENCES

What is abundantly clear is that while more information continues to become available electronically, license agreements impede a library's ability to provide access to that same electronic information. As is evident from the examination of various libraries' mission statements, a main goal of most academic libraries is to provide broad access to resources, whether print or electronic, for all its patrons. While the library may have set forth a mission of providing broad-based access to all resources for its patrons, it will often not be able to meet those goals due to the various licensing agreements into which it has entered.

These license agreements impede a library's ability to provide access in a number of ways. One main way licenses curtail access is through the definition of authorized user. Alumni, a group generally not specifically listed in the definition of authorized user, are an important group in supporting the library post-graduation (Horava, 2007). As a result, many libraries commit to providing alumni access to their resources. Some libraries continue to allow full or limited borrowing from the print collection, reference support, and access to electronic resources (Horava). However, while libraries are promising broad access to the library's resources for alumni, in many instances the library is unable to provide access to its electronic resources for this group unless they are willing to utilize the resource on-site at the library. This may be impossible for alumni who have relocated or not ideal for alumni who prefer to access information from wherever they are at any given moment. Additionally, alumni are often not familiar with the implications of license agreements and the ways in which they limit access to various user groups. Due to these impediments to access, alumni may become frustrated and less willing to support the library after graduation if they believe promises cannot be honored.

Another way in which license agreements impact the library's ability to provide access to patrons is by stipulating that authorized users can only access the electronic database while on-site at the library or the greater institution. As a result of this type of restriction, authorized users cannot access information at their convenience from any location. This type of site restriction significantly affects users who expect electronic information to be available to them at all times no matter where they are. It also has the potential to impact institutions and they way in which they provide access to their distance students. If a license agreement does not allow for off-site access, distance students may be denied the ability to access materials needed for their educational experience.

License agreements also impinge on a library's ability to provide access by restricting or eliminating various copyright privileges that a library would normally be entitled to rely on. License agreements often eliminate the library's right to engage in interlibrary loan transactions. One primary reason that database vendors eliminate a library's ability to engage in interlibrary loan transactions is for economic reasons. If the database vendor allows libraries to engage in interlibrary loan, the vendor may lose substantial dollars because a third party who might choose to enter into a license with the vendor no longer needs to do so since they can simply request the same material via interlibrary loan. By eliminating this ability, the library will no longer be able to serve outside patrons. Thus, the library cannot provide access to other institutions and their patrons, and once again access has been severely impeded by the license agreement.

A related problem as a result of these proprietary electronic databases is their ability to limit access to information to those persons who are independent researchers or scholars. Since these persons are considered non-affiliates of the university they are relegated to only obtaining access to information as a walk-in patron, if that is permitted at the institution, or by possibly paying out of pocket for such access. As is the case with many private institutions, the only people permitted on-site access to the library and its resources are current students, faculty, and staff. On occasion, these institutions may permit continued access by alumni, but that is not always the case. Additionally, these institutions often do not permit access to the library for public patrons and in those circumstances when they do, the public patron must pay a daily use fee to work on-site at the library. In the past, when the majority of content was available in print form, these patrons could request the material through interlibrary loan and access it in that manner without suffering monetary penalties. However, with the advent of strict licensing agreements, libraries are often not permitted to engage in interlibrary loan of electronic content and resources. As a result, a whole segment of the population, independent researchers and scholars, are denied access to pertinent information (Wand, 2005).

As a result of these license agreement restrictions, libraries and their librarians may look for creative ways to continue to provide access to all their patrons. In some cases, librarians attempt to work around the terms and limitations of the license agreement by performing a search in the electronic database for a patron. Due to the fact that librarians are permitted access to that electronic database, they believe that engaging in a search for a patron who does not fall within the definition of authorized user is acceptable. However, by engaging in this type of activity the library may very well be in breach of its license agreement.

What is apparent is that no matter the library's goals and mission, it is unlikely that it will truly be able to live up to those statements as a result of the limitations imposed by license agreements. While some licenses may impose greater restrictions or limitations than others, most license agreements will impede a library's ability to provide access to its patrons in one form or another. While these impediments to access may seem small if looked at individually, when examined in the aggregate, they are large and significant. In a world where more and more information can only be accessed electronically, if license agreements continue to impede libraries' abilities to provide access to all its patrons, the divide between those people who have access to electronic databases and their content and those people who do not will only continue to grow.

CONCLUSION

A core value of librarianship, equal access for all users, is challenged by this shift to electronic content and the resulting license agreement structure. It is essential that libraries pay closer attention to this issue of access to electronic information. Libraries should be greatly concerned with continuing to provide the same level of access to their patrons as was available before the advent of and continual shift to electronic resources. Unfortunately, the nature of licensing agreements is preventing libraries from doing just that. In this era of Google, instant messaging, and instant access, many library patrons want access to everything from wherever they are located at that given time (Horava, 2007). However, this shift to electronic delivery of information actually impedes access for many patrons of the library. Database vendors have the ability to restrict and control access to their information as a result of the same electronic and instant access technology on which many library patrons have come to rely (Bartow, 2001).

Libraries must engage in close scrutiny of every license agreement into which they enter. They must determine how the various provisions of the license will impinge on their ability to provide access to patrons, whether their primary constituency or those that fall outside of the group, such as other higher education institutions, alumni, and the public. In particular, attention must be paid to the provisions that impact the library's right to engage in fair use of copyrighted materials and its ability to engage in interlibrary loan transactions. These rights have become implicit when considering print materials, yet are often amorphous when dealing with electronic resources. Access to electronic information will continue to be more limited as we move into the future unless libraries begin making changes to the terms of the license agreements that they enter into for electronic content.

In order to provide broad-based access for all its patrons, libraries must continue to fight for these rights. The first step in this fight is to negotiate license agreement terms that allow the library to provide broader access or to negotiate for the purchase of the electronic content as opposed to the licensing or leasing of such content. It will take a coalition of libraries acting as a unified front to begin this process of change. Currently, database vendors hold the upper hand and have the ability to force their terms of access upon libraries. Were libraries to present a more unified front and require database vendors to provide access on their terms, a shift may begin to take place. Then the libraries may find themselves the more powerful party in the licensing arrangement.

An example of libraries unifying is the "Shared E-Resource Understanding" (SERU) project. Recently, a coalition of 21 librarians and 8 publishers agreed to use the SERU document, which sets forth a list of points by which each side agrees to abide (Glenn, 2007). The parties participating in this pilot initiative agree to deal in good faith if or when a dispute arises between them and to abide by a list of stipulated guidelines or understandings with the only legally binding contract being the purchase order (Glenn). This project is still in its infancy and the publishers participating include an open access journal publisher and university presses. It remains to be seen whether this idea will work and if it could be transitioned into and implemented by large database vendors in licensing agreement situations.

"Today, when the Web gives society the illusion that all information is available to everyone, more and more of the latest and most highly vetted research findings are locked up in expensive, proprietary databases accessible by fewer and fewer individuals" (Wand, 2005, p. 30). We, as a society, must have access to this electronic content in order to contribute to new knowledge and thinking (Wand). Libraries must persevere in their efforts to provide access to electronic resources for all their patrons. If not, access will continue to become more and more limited and huge segments of the population will be unable to access much needed resources and knowledge. Libraries cannot rely on others, particularly database vendors, to provide current and on-going access to the information locked away in electronic databases. The party who cares about access and is willing to provide access to all users is the library. In order to meet their goals and missions, libraries must step to the forefront in the fight against the contemptible limitations that database vendors impose with their license agreements.

REFERENCES

American Library Association Access to Electronic Information, Services, and Networks: An Interpretation of the Library Bill of Rights. Retrieved October 2, 2007, from http://www.ala.org/Template.cfm?Section=interpretations&Template=/ContentManagement/ContentDisplay.cfm&ContentID=133993

American Library Association Core Values of Librarianship. Retrieved October 2, 2007, from.http://www.ala.org/ala/oif/statementspols/corevaluesstatement/corevalues.htm

Bartow, A. (2001). Libraries in a digital and aggressively copyrighted world: Retaining patron access through changing technologies. *Ohio State Law Journal, 62,* 821-834.

Glenn, D. (2007, September 21). Librarians and publishers try out a plan to simplify negotiations over electronic resources. *The Chronicle of Higher Education.* Retrieved September 21, 2007, from http://0-chronicle.com.bianca.penlib.du.edu/daily/2007/09/2007092103n.htm

Harris, L. E. (2002). *Licensing digital content: A practical guide for librarians.* Chicago: American Library Association.

Horava, T. (2007). Licensing e-resources for alumni: Reflections from a pilot project. *College & Research Libraries News, July/August,* 437-441.

Johnson, P. (2004). *Fundamentals of collection development & management.* Chicago: American Library Association.

Klinefelter, A. (2001). Copyright and electronic library resources: An overview of how the law is affecting traditional library services. *Legal Reference Services Quarterly, 19,* 175-193.

Lowry, A. (1993). Landlords and tenants: Who owns information, who pays for it, and how? *Serials Librarian, 23(3-4)*, 61-71.

Mission of the Auraria Library. Retrieved September 26, 2007, from http://library/auraria.edu/aboutus/whoweare/mission.html

Regis University Libraries Mission Statement. Retrieved September 26, 2007, from http://www.regis.edu/library.asp?page=about.overview.mission

Reitz, J. M. (Ed.). (2004). *Dictionary for library and information science.* Westport, CT: Libraries Unlimited.

Roether, D., & Koepf, L. (2005). Information may become freely available, but information is not free, *Best Practices, Winter,* 1-5.

United States Copyright Act, 17 U.S.C.A. §107 (ThomsonWest 2005).

United States Copyright Act, 17 U.S.C.A. §108 (ThomsonWest 2005).

United States Copyright Act, 17 U.S.C.A. §109 (ThomsonWest 2005).

University of Colorado at Boulder University Libraries Mission Statement. Retrieved August 12, 2007, from http://uclibraries.colorado.edu/dea/mission.htm

University of Colorado Law Library Collection Development Policy. Retrieved September 26, 2007, from http://www.colorado.edu/Law/lawlib/ts/index_print.htm

University of Denver Penrose Library Frequently Asked Questions. Retrieved August 12, 2007, from http://penrose.du.edu/FindIt/HelpWithResearch/FAQ/index.cfm?id1=1@id3=47

Wallenius, L. I. T. (2007). Are electronic serials helping or hindering academic libraries? *Acquisitions Librarian, 19,* 75-82.

Wand, P. (2005). On my mind: Inaccessible information: A strategic solution. *American Libraries, 36(5),* 30.

Westminster Law Library Mission Statement. Retrieved August 12, 2007, from http://www.law.du.edu/library/content.cfm?pg=mission

In: Academic Librarianship in the 21st Century ISBN: 978-1-60456-865-3
Editors: C. M.Garcia and T. A.Flores

Chapter 2

USERS' INFORMATION NEEDS IN ACADEMIC LIBRARIES OF THE 21ST CENTURY: ASSESSMENT OF THE LIBQUAL+TM TOOLS IN IMPROVING SERVICE QUALITY STANDARDS

Maria Anna Jankowska
Social Sciences Librarian, Charles E. Young Research Library
UCLA, Los Angeles, California, USA

Google Scholar, Amazon.com, Wikiepedia, Flicker, MySpace, social networking, open access, and easy retrieval of electronic resources and services create higher user expectations for an academic library's collections and services. In this competitive environment of content providers and users' growing expectations, academic libraries face a difficult task in providing the most satisfying ways of delivering information and services to their patrons. To what extent should academic libraries recognize the users' information needs in the areas of service and collections? Is it possible for libraries to fulfill users' growing expectations toward libraries' collections and services? What would happen if Google failed?

In searching for answers to these questions this article not only presents the LibQUAL +TM survey results that helped to determine users' satisfaction and expectations of the quality of library service, but it also evaluates the outcomes of the survey that were implemented to improve the quality of offered library services. Assessment of service quality standards by library users is becoming a crucial element in future advances taking place in academic libraries. These advances will not only influence the quality of offered services but also determine the new formats of services. They will create demand for new organizational and spatial libraries' structure, cooperation, and integrated services, which will better fulfill educational and research university missions.

For more than 2000 years people have considered libraries as treasures of knowledge, information, and cultures. Their educational and cultural values rested in the contents of library collections. Nevertheless, in this day of prime digital information formats and communication technologies libraries are constantly losing their collection content, which is being intercepted by commercial stockholders such as Google Book Project, Google Scholar, Amazon.com Look Inside, and Microsoft's Windows Live Book Search. Fast development of open access publishing models has provided free and wide access to scholarly resources that were entirely inaccessible to all users years ago. Additionally, Web 2.0 has contributed to easy distribution and exchange of content in forms of text, images, and multimedia through the growing fast social-networking environment of blogs, podcasts, Wikis, MySpace, Facebook, YouTube, and Flicker.

In December 2004, the main task of Google Library Project was to digitize five big collections available in Stanford University, the University of Michigan, Harvard University, Oxford University and the New York Public Library. Two years later, the main group of five universities has been enlarged by additional collections from the University of California, the University of Wisconsin-Madison, University of Virginia, and Madrid's Complutense University [1]. Some libraries participating in the Google Library Project have already been active in other digitizing projects such as Open Content Alliance organized by the Internet Archive, Yahoo, and Microsoft.

These enormous digitized collections will enable users' access, searching, and retrieval of their content available not only in text but also in multimedia materials. Fast and easy retrieval of digitized content with commercial services has created higher user expectations toward academic libraries' collections and services. In the competitive environment of commercial content providers and growing expectations from users, academic libraries are facing difficult tasks in providing the most satisfying ways of delivering different formats of content and services to their patrons.

The dynamics of technological conversions are providing wide variety of choices for content distribution while satisfying the information needs of a growing number of users. Additionally, commercial competitive initiatives have mobilized libraries to pay more attention not only to statistical measurements evaluating their operations, but also to measurements of their effectiveness expressed in quality of library services. Prominent literature on this subject stressed the fact that proper evaluation of library work by users helps libraries in the realization of definite goals, alleviation of users' informational expectations, and deliberation of higher quality services [2].

This article presents the results of the 2004 University of Idaho (UI) Library's LibQUAL+ TM survey on growing informational needs of users in the academic library. Additionally, the article also evaluates the effectiveness of the LibQUAL+ TM recommendations that were implemented in the UI Library to achieve higher user satisfactions. In the entire evaluation process of satisfying information needs of academic users one should ask the following questions:

- To what extent should academic libraries alleviate the growing informational requirements of their users?
- Should academic libraries seek to alleviate only the teaching and scientific information needs of their users or address other interests as well?
- What would happen if Google, Yahoo, Wikipedia, and Microsoft failed in their attempt to provide content that supports the informational needs of academic users?
- Is it possible for libraries to satisfy users' growing expectations toward library collections and services without losing their central function as treasures of knowledge, information, and culture?

In seeking answers to the questions mentioned above one must consider not only new solutions resulting from information and communications technologies but also the satisfaction of users and their hard-to-predict habits and behaviors in searching, processing, and utilization of data and information.

INTERNATIONAL USERS' OPINIONS ABOUT THE VISION OF THE LIBRARY

The OCLC international research report on users' perceptions of library and information sources published in 2005 stressed the fact that 84% of respondents start their information search from using free Web search engines [3]. Only one percent of information consumers begin their research by going to a library Web site. They valued free available search engines on the Web more than the abilities of librarians to help them in searching for needed information. Only six-percent of respondents were satisfied with the quality of services received in their libraries. However, the majority of respondents were not aware of available commercial databases and electronic resources purchased by libraries in order to help them in their information seeking and retrieving process. Information consumers view library as a quiet place to study with access to free information and friendly personnel. The OCLC survey findings stressed the fact that users still consider printed books as the main source of information in libraries and they are not aware of the amount of electronic resources available in today's libraries. At the beginning of the 21st century, the printed book is still considered as the library brand.

Findings from the OCLC report as well as postulates coming from review of comprehensive literature about behaviors of information users proves that libraries in their strategic planning should strongly emphasize users' growing information needs [4]. Interesting is the fact that some OCLC findings were similar to findings from the UI Library's LibQUAL+ TM survey from 2004. One of the findings for example was users' unawareness of full range of the UI Library new services and resources.

THE LIBQUAL+ TM SURVEY INSTRUMENTS

The UI Library was among 202 libraries in the United States, Canada and Europe that participated in the 2004 LibQUAL + TM survey as part of the American Association of Research Libraries (ARL) measures initiative. This web-based survey evaluated users' perception and expectation of their library's service quality by measuring the gaps between minimal, desired and perceived levels of service [5]. The UI Library users marked on a Lickert scale (from 1 to 9 where 9 was the most preferable) the 22 LibQUAL +TM responses to questions associated with the library service quality in three dimensions:

- Affect of Service (AS): measures the human aspect of library services (readiness and willingness to help users, and the knowledge to answer users' questions, etc.)
- Information Control (IC): measures ability to navigate library resources independently (access to print and electronic resources, library website, document delivery, comprehensive collections, convenient business hours, etc.)
- Library as Place (LP): measures the library environment and location (space, comfort, learning environment).

The survey results were compared nationally across academic libraries and they not only measured satisfaction with the UI Library services but also guided the Library in planning new and improving existing services and collections.

USER POPULATION AND RESPONDENTS

A group of 2,700 of the UI Library users (600 faculty, 600 staff, 900 undergraduate and 600 graduate students) was randomly selected by the Institutional Research and Assessment Office (Library faculty and staff were excluded). Between March and April of 2004 all members of this group received up to three invitations from the Library dean to participate in the LibQUAL +TM survey by filling out a Web questionnaire. The final sample size measured by the number of valid surveys returned was 571 users, for an effective response rate of 21%. Among the user groups, undergraduate students represented the largest group of respondents (40.5%), next were graduate students (33.7%), then faculty (18.6%), and staff (7.2%). Individuals from all four groups of users also provided 275 useful written comments, which were analyzed and used in the Library's future planning. Among the user population, 56% were identified as male and 44% as female. Thirty percent of the users were age 18 to 22, 29% were age 23 to 30, 22% were age 31-45, 19% were age 46-65. Users were identified as being in one of four discipline categories: users within sciences represented 43.3% of the respondents, users in the social sciences 33.6%, in the humanities 12.7%, and in the fourth category (general studies, undecided, etc.) 10.4% [6].

ASSESSMENT RESULTS

Results from the LibQUAL +TM survey determined the gaps between users' perceived level of library services and their desired level (superiority gaps). The gaps were calculated in three dimensions: Information Control (IC), Affect of Services (AS) and Library as Place (LP). Calculated statistical means for all 22 questions in these three dimensions presented the highest "desired mean" (which expresses users' greatest priorities), highest "perceived mean" (Library's greatest strengths), lowest "superiority mean" (users' greatest satisfaction with Library services), and the highest "superiority mean" (greatest dissatisfactions with Library services, signifying areas for improvement). These four means are represented in Table 1 by answers from the survey that received the highest rankings for the entire population of respondents and subsequently for each of four user groups.

For all user groups the *greatest priorities* were in the Information Control dimension. The highest "Greatest Strengths" in the "All Users" group was reached for those survey questions related to a library Web site that would enable users easily locate information themselves (desired mean 8.28) and the availability of the print and electronic journals that users required for their work (desired mean 8.22). The faculty group expressed the same priorities but in reverse order. Undergraduate students stressed modern equipment and a library Web site enabling them to access information on their own as their main priorities. An easy to navigate library Website was also among the greatest priorities for the graduate students, who also expressed their interest in making electronic resources accessible from home and office.

Both graduate students and faculty stressed the importance of library's employees who give users individual attention and are knowledgeable enough to answer their questions. Graduate students and faculty responded that employees who were consistently courteous and ready to respond to users' questions were among the *library's greatest strengths*. Undergraduate students considered modern equipment that lets them easily assess information on their own and the availability of quiet space in the library for individual activities as the library's greatest strengths.

The greatest satisfactions among library users were in the "Affect of Services" and "Library as Place" dimensions. The patrons were satisfied that library employees give them individual attention and treat them in a caring fashion. Additionally, all users were very satisfied with the library as a community space for group learning, group study, and as a quiet space for study.

The superiority mean measured the gap between users' minimal, desired level of service and their perceived level of service indicating the areas of greatest dissatisfaction in library service. *The highest dissatisfactions* for the users as a whole were in the "Information Control" dimension. Having the print and/or electronic journals that users require for their work scored the highest superiority mean among faculty (gap –2.31), graduate students (-1.76), staff (-1.60), and all users (-1.49). Making electronic resources accessible from home and office scored as the second biggest superiority gap by both undergraduate (-0.97) and graduate (-1.47) students and faculty (-1.67). Library employees who instill confidence in users scored the highest superiority mean (-0.98) among undergraduate students.

Table 1. Answers from the survey by three dimensions (IC – Information Control, AS - Affect of Service, LP – Library as Place) that received the highest rankings for the entire population of respondents and for each of four user groups

Dimension	Greatest Priorities	Greatest Strengths	Greatest Satisfactions	Greatest Dissatisfactions
All Users				
IC	Library website enabling me to locate information on my own. Print and/or electronic journal collections I require for my work.			Print and/or electronic journal collections I require for my work. Making electronic resources accessible from my home or office.
AS		Employees who are consistently courteous. Readiness to respond to users' questions.	Giving users individual attention. Employees who deal with users in a caring fashion.	
LP			Community space for group learning and group study. Quiet space for individual activities.	

Table 1. (Continued)

Undergraduate Students				
IC	Modern equipment that lets me easily access information on my own. Library website enabling me to locate information on my own	Modern equipment that lets me easily access information on my own.		Making electronic resources accessible from my home or office.
AS			Willingness to help users. Employees who deal with users in a caring fashion.	Employees who instill confidence in users.
LP		Quiet space for individual activities.		
Graduate Students				
IC	Making electronic resources accessible from my home or office. Library website enabling me to locate information on my own.	Modern equipment that lets me easily access information on my own.		Print and/or electronic journal collections I require for my work. Making electronic resources accessible from my home or office.
AS	Giving users individual attention.	Employees who are consistently courteous. Readiness to respond to users' questions.	Giving users individual attention.	
LP			Community space for group learning and group study.	

Table 1. (Continued)

Faculty				
Dimension	Greatest Priorities	Greatest Strengths	Greatest Satisfactions	Greatest Dissatisfactions
IC	Print and/or electronic journal collections I require for my work. Library website enabling me to locate information on my own.			Print and/or electronic journal collections I require for my work. Making electronic resources accessible from my home or office
AS	Employees who have the knowledge to answer users' questions.	Employees who are consistently courteous. Giving users individual attention.	Giving users individual attention.	
LP			Quiet space for individual activities.	
Staff				
IC	Library website enabling me to locate information on my own.			Print and/or electronic journal collections I require for my work. Making information easily accessible for independent use.
AS	Employees who are consistently courteous. Dependability in handling users' service problems.	Readiness to respond to users' questions. Employees who are consistently courteous.		Employees who understand the needs of their users.
LP			Quiet space for individual activities. Community space for group learning and group study.	

KEY FINDINGS OF THE SURVEY

An interpretation of the survey responses lead to the following conclusions:

- The human aspect of the library services was the greatest strength of the UI Library.
- All users highly value the library as a comfortable community space for group learning and a quiet place to study.
- The inadequacy of the print and electronic journal collection to support learning and research in all disciplines and the difficulty finding electronic databases and resources were perceived as the greatest weaknesses of the library.
- Improving navigation of the library Web site, increasing the print and electronic journal collections, and better marketing of available resources were perceived as the greatest priorities for the library.
- Library users expected the library to help them find, use, and evaluate information in order to stay abreast in their disciplines by creating more online tutorials, resources, subject guides, and information literacy instruction.
- Overall the UI Library scored higher in user perceptions (7.01 perceived mean) than the other 202 academic libraries in the United States and abroad. In two dimensions, "Affect of Services" and "Library as Place", the UI Library perceived means were higher than many other libraries. The users highly valued the library's helpful, knowledgeable, courteous employees and a comfortable learning environment in the library. Only in the Information Control dimension the UI Library perceived mean (6.99) was lower than in the other 202 libraries (7.01). The lower mean for the UI Library was the result of student (both graduate and undergraduate) and faculty dissatisfaction from not having sufficient print and electronic journal collections for their study, teaching and research, lack of modern equipment, and the need for a library Web site design that would make information more easily available and enable them to locate information themselves.

Implementation of LibQUAL+TM Survey Results

The findings and written comments from the LibQUAL+TM survey suggested that UI Library users expected improvements in dimensions of services, collections, and in the library building. Therefore, the library took the following actions:

- Expanded access to scientific e-journals,
- Improved access to print and electronic journal holdings by implementing a "current journal list" and an Open URL resolver,
- Obtained subscriptions to the Web of Science JSTOR database, the IEE, IEEE conference proceedings, and others,
- Redesigned the library home page by adding new online services for specific users category such as faculty and graduate students,
- Added to the library's website number of help guides, tutorials, and pathfinders,
- Targeted instruction for graduate students, including classes on bibliographic managers and subject-specific databases,
- Advertised all new library acquisition on both the UI and the library web sites,
- Purchased new photocopy machine and furniture for the library.

All listed actions helped the UI Library enlarge its collection of electronic journals and provided better access to the entire collection by improving navigation of the library website. Additionally, the library faculties have created new online instructions and tutorials, increased awareness of library services and resources, and improved the quality of study areas in the library building, helping the UI Library to overcome weaknesses stressed by its users.

Conclusions

Two years after implementing these changes the UI Library users have been mostly satisfied with the library's technological and organizational improvements as reported by the exit graduate student surveys. However, today the users are asking for more. The architecture students in their class projects worked on designing future information commons in the library. They presented the library as very comfortable place to study with modern furniture, fireplace, coffee place, colorful walls, carpets, computer stations, and a wide range of multimedia equipment.

In response to four research questions driving the evaluation process of satisfying information needs of academic users, it is worth considering the following.

- Academic libraries wishing to keep up with users' growing expectations require constant assessments of their service quality. User feedback is becoming a standard evaluation mechanism for improving the quality of academic library collections, services, and buildings. In striving to satisfy users' growing information needs academic libraries are facing technological, economic and organizational challenges.
- Academic libraries can only afford to satisfy those user information needs that support the core academic functions including teaching and scholarly information needs. Through proper marketing of their collections and services and educating their users, academic libraries are able to shape and influence users' expectations towards their services and collections.
- Google Scholar, Google Book Project, Wikipedia, Amazon.com Look Inside, Microsoft's Window Live Book Search, and Open Access scholarship will continue to provide digital content to academic users. All of these commercial stakeholders are quite young competitors to the historically established libraries with more then 2000 year traditions. Academic libraries are not well equipped to compete with the commercial entities but in their strategic planning they should always be ready to handle situations where commercial entities fail to provide quality content to academic users.
- The educational and cultural values of academic libraries are the result of both the content included in their collections and their services to users offered by professional staff. In this age of digital information formats and communications technologies libraries have been losing their collection content to the commercial stockholders, but they are still able to provide their special brand of service to users that no on-line providers can offer. By focusing on providing high quality services that satisfy users' growing information needs, academic libraries will be able to keep their central function as stockpiles of knowledge, information and culture. To keep this central function in the 21st century academic libraries should concentrate on providing the best quality of existing services, creating new ones, designing new organizational and spatial

structures, cooperation, and integrating services to effectively fulfill educational and research universities' missions.

REFERENCES AND NOTES

[1] Herring M. Y.: *Don't Get Goggle-Eyed Over Google's Plan to Digitize.* The Chronicle of Higher Education 2005 nr 51 (27): B20 http://books.google.com/ googlebooks /partners.html

[2] Yvonna S. Lincoln. "Insights into Library Services and Users from Qualitative Research," *Library and Information Science Research,* 24 (2002):10; Colleen Cook and Fred Heath, "Users' Perceptions of Library Service Quality: a LibQUAL+TM Qualitative Study," *Library Trends* 49, no. 4 (Spring 2001): 553;

[3] *Perceptions of Libraries and Information Resources* [online] [26.08.2006]. Dublin, OH: OCLC, 2005. http://www.oclc.org/reports/2005perceptions.htm

[4] Jankowska M.: *Identifying University Professors' Information Needs in the Challenging Environment of Information and Communication Technologies. Journal of Academic Librarianship* 2004 nr 31 (1), s. 51-66

[5] More information about LibQUAL see: *LibQUAL – Charting Library Service Quality* [online] http://www.libqual.org/index.cfm

[6] Hernon P., Calvert P. J.: *Methods for Measuring Service Quality in Libraries in New Zealand. Journal of Academic Librarianship* 1997 nr 22(5), s. 387.

In: Academic Librarianship in the 21st Century ISBN: 978-1-60456-865-3
Editors: C. M.Garcia and T. A.Flores

Chapter 3

BIBLIOGRAPHIC MANAGEMENT SOFTWARE AND Z39.50 CONNECTION IN THAI ACADEMIC LIBRARIES

Aurathai Wareesa-ard*

Lecturer, Library and Information Science Department,
Faculty of Humanities, Srinakharinwirot University, Thailand

ABSTRACT

This paper is based on a research, Use of the EndNote program for bibliographic management in Srinakharinwirot University's style manual. It describes the situation in Thailand in which bibliographic management software such as EndNote is rarely known and used as a research tool in the academic setting. This situation is caused by the limitation of EndNote as it cannot support Thai language, and is partly caused by the fact that most Thai universities established their own style manuals. The paper reports a study being carried out to solve the problem. In this study, templates for Srinakharinwirot University (SWU) style manual were constructed for creating bibliographies by using EndNote program. Z39.50 connection files for Thai academic libraries were created and tested. This development enables library patrons to access, download, retrieve and import bibliographic records from the databases of academic universities and manage their bibliographies more efficiently and conveniently. Lastly, the

*Srinakharinwirot University, Sukhumvit 23, Bangkok 10110, Thailand Tel. 662-6495577 Fax: 662-2600122 Email: aurathai@swu.ac.th aurathaiw@gmail.com

author emphasizes the important roles of academic libraries in Thailand in promoting the use of bibliographic management software by providing needed facilities and organizing training courses for faculties, students and researchers.

INTRODUCTION

In writing academic papers, it is necessary to develop good academic practice of citing information sources one used and list them in the reference/bibliography. Whether the author quotes from other people's work or get some ideas from others and present them in his/her paper, credit must be given to the owners of the work. This is called "citations." Citations support readers to locate and examine sources used, show scope of the research, and display the evidence of what is the author's work and what the author derived from other work/research. Citations also append credibility to the author's work by showing that he/she has studied and searched from a variety of resources. The important concept attached to the practice is "being ethical in research." Thus, the word "plagiarism" is known in the academic world "when a writer intentionally uses someone else's language, ideas, or other original (not common-knowledge) material without acknowledging its source." [1] In fact, most people do not intend to plagiarize, but they do not cite sources because they are not aware of good academic practice which emphasizes academic integrity and do not know how to do citations. It is, therefore, important to create this awareness among academicians and introduce to them various standard citation/ reference/ bibliography formats and rules so that they can use it properly.

In Thailand, both Thai and English languages are used in academic writing. In citing sources in English, authors can choose from several style manuals that are widely used internationally, such as APA, MLA, Chicago, Vancouver, etc. However, there is no standard format for citing sources in Thai. Some universities established their own style manuals for both Thai and English citations. Srinakharinwirot University (SWU) is one that created a style manual in 1961 and has had it revised periodically in 1971, 1978, 1980, 1987, 1991, 2003, and 2004. The SWU style manual is incorporated in LIS 101 Information Literacy Skills course, which is compulsory for year one undergraduate students. The style manual is also published and distributed to graduate students and faculty members. However, the bibliographic management software, widely used in many countries, especially Australia and New Zealand, is not yet known as a valuable tool in Thailand.

This article is based on a research paper, "Use of the EndNote program for bibliographic management in Srinakharinwirot University's style." The research proposes the application of EndNote version 9.0 for managing bibliographies both in Thai and English according to the SWU style manual. In addition it attempts to create the Z39.50 connection files for academic libraries in Thailand so that users can access and download bibliographic records from other university libraries' databases. [2]

PROBLEM STATEMENT

In Thailand, there are 80 public universities all around the country. They are under the authority of the Ministry of Education. The academic libraries are deemed important to higher education. For over the last two decades, the libraries have steadily progressed and have been well supported by the government. They became much more developed than other types of libraries in Thailand, especially in their services and technology. [3]

Since 1975, all public academic libraries have participated in a cooperative program, which is aimed towards sharing resources and taking joint action to carry out activities, such as acquisitions, cataloguing, serials, information services, media services, and information technology. In 1994, Chulalongkorn University started its library automation system using INNOPAC software. Later on other universities had gradually automated their library systems. Different integrated library software such as INNOPAC, HORIZON and VTLS, being customized for Thai users, are used by academic libraries.

In 1997, the UniNet (Inter-University Network) was set up by the Office of Information Technology Administration for Educational Development, the Ministry of University Affairs (now the Commission of Higher Education within the Ministry of Education). The UniNet provides the national and international network services for all universities and higher education institutions in Thailand. Academic libraries across the country are linked via UniNet. [4]

At present, the integrated library program of most libraries, especially the Online Public Access Catalogue is upgraded to the Graphic mode or WEBPAC. The libraries also create their web sites to enable access to library resources and services via internet.

However, the bibliographic management software is not yet available through any academic library WEBPAC. Users have to copy or save or send by email the needed bibliographic records in formats such as html or plain text, and manually put them in a standard format of bibliography. Some library catalogs provide menu formats for selecting style manuals such as MLA and Chicago, but in fact they are not available. Library automation systems and network technology are not yet at a well-developed stage in some libraries, so the systems cannot fully support all functions of library software.

Currently a few scholars use bibliographic management software in searching and importing records through Z39.50 connection directly, except for the Thai language materials because most software does not support Thai language. The language is one of the barriers in using bibliographic management software. Over half of academic library collections consist of Thai language materials, but Thai scripts cannot be read or interpreted by such software. Therefore, the research on "Use of the EndNote program for bibliographic management in Srinakharinwirot University's style" is carried out to solve the problem.

Bibliographic Management Software

Bibliographic management software is also known as personal bibliographic manager (PBM), personal bibliographic software, personal bibliographic database, bibliographic software, and reference manager. It was developed to help scholars and students manage citations, retrieve bibliographical information to create bibliographies in a variety of styles. Presently, the most popular programs include EndNote, ProCite, and Reference Manager. [5] These programs are designed to be easy to use. Users can key in citations manually or search from other library catalogs and import citations directly into their personal files/databases. Besides, more than one thousand of international journal styles are provided for creating bibliographies in articles.

The software allow users to search all references by several access points such as author, title, journal title, and keywords, and to insert selected references into Word documents easily. Since the bibliographic management software can be integrated with word processing program which produces a reference list in the appropriate format automatically, it is called that *"Cite While You Write"* (CWYW). [6] Unlimited number of bibliographic records can be conveniently stored in any personal computer. Currently, most bibliographic management software is integrated with Z39.50 technology, so it serves as a gateway to the world of information resources. [7]

Z39.50 Connection

Z39.50 is a computer-to-computer communications protocol or searching protocol. It is a NISO (National Information Standards Organization) standard for searching and retrieving of data (bibliographic records). It allows searching of databases and multiple server databases via one user client. It is designed to work specially with text databases. In the internet age, Z39.50 has become much more important because it is a tool for one user client to search and retrieve information from various computer systems. Database providers are very interested in Z39.50, because it allows customers to access their information via Z39.50 conveniently and quickly. Researchers are excited by the power of Z39.50. They can search multiple databases in a few clicks in order to access the great library collections of the world. In addition, they can retrieve abstracts of articles from journals in various subject fields. [8]

Although the Z39.50 standard facilitates access to all types of data, not every client or server can support this standard. Fortunately, many user interfaces and database servers were recently designed and developed to support Z39.50 standard. In the library community, Z39.50 standard has an obvious role to broadcast searching and union catalog. This means users can search from multiple library catalogs in one click. In the same manner, bibliographic management software such as EndNote program can apply Z39.50 standard to enable searching, collecting, and importing bibliographic records from multiple library catalogs and online databases.

Literature Review

This article reviews some of the literature on bibliographic management and Z39.50 Connection with the emphasis on their value benefited by scholars and students in academic institutions. Kunin (1985) used microcomputers to manage citations and bibliographies. The dBASE II program was applied to create bibliographic databases; store and retrieve data using keywords and Boolean operators; collect references and arrange them in alphabetical order or by subject heading; and print bibliographic lists. This program was able to facilitate quick retrieval of bibliographic records and manage large collections of citations. [9]

Hitoshi Sato, Satomi Sato and Horikoshi (1996) developed a bibliographic management program called MacRefer, by using Macintosh personal computers. MacRefer was able to search and import bibliographic records from online databases and create various reference styles. It could perform special advanced searches by combining up to nine keywords for any data field with the results and search conditions preserved. However, when compared with EndNote Plus, MacRefer is not as accommodating to users due to several limitations. For example, MacRefer can store only 10,000 references while EndNote Plus can store over 30,000 references. [10]

East (2003), who was an Interlibrary Loan Service librarian at Queensland University Library, in Australia, found that many scholars used bibliographic management software such as EndNote, Reference Manager, and ProCite to search and access the bibliographic records via Z39.50 standard. By using EndNote program, scholars could directly access various online databases and download bibliographic records. However, some problems occurred in searching via Z39.50 connection from some standard library automation software such as Innovative Interfaces, GEAC, SIRSI and Endeavour, and from two online databases vendors: Research Libraries Group and SilverPlatter. East found that software developers or vendors selected different search options to implement the standard differently in their systems. For example, some vendors used incorrect or inadequate search attributes, thus the searchers received false records or could not retrieve records although they existed in the database. Besides, the lack of uniformity in database indexing was a big problem that affected search performances.

In spite of such limitations, East maintained that using bibliographic management software through Z39.50 searching standard was very useful to scholars. He suggested that libraries improve the effectiveness of Z39.50 standard as a research tool. He reported that most academic libraries in Australia promoted the application of EndNote program extensively. They also provided 2- to 3-hour EndNote training courses to library patrons. [11]

Krooden (2004) found that most universities in Southern Africa could not afford to buy microcomputers or any commercial bibliographic management software. Therefore, he tried to apply word processing software to create a personal bibliographic database. The training workshop was organized for the graduate students who registered for a module named Research Information Skills (RIS) at the University of South Africa (UNISA). Krooden described the advantages and disadvantages of word processing software in managing the bibliographies and compared it with other bibliographic management software [12]

Gall and Brahmi (2004) tested the capability of the EndNote version 7.0 for searching and importing bibliographic records from MEDLINE database into EndNote. Findings revealed that users preferred searching MEDLINE directly to searching via EndNote. Users found that EndNote lacked the limit search feature for advanced search options, such as searching limits by publication date. Apart from that, it took a long time to download search results when they connected from EndNote to MEDLINE database. Thomson ISI Researchsoft, who produced EndNote, also pointed out some limitations of EndNote in searching external databases. [13]

McGeachin (2004) studied the information-seeking behavior of scholars and their bibliographic management. He found that many scholars used bibliographic management software in importing citations from online databases to create bibliographies. He then recommended that the libraries support scholars in using bibliographic management software effectively. [14]

Kessler and Van Ullen (2005) found that most librarians being studied supported the use of bibliographic management software, especially EndNote program which had been widely used among the faculties and graduate students. However, EndNote was very expensive for students. Therefore, Kessler and Van Ullen compared 3 programs: EndNote, EasyBib and NoodleBib, with an attempt to find the most accurate, user-friendly, and suitable software in the undergraduate environment. They concluded that EndNote was commercial software which was more complex than the other two. It was designed for researchers, faculties and graduate students who needed to be familiarized with its operation. In contrast, EasyBib and NoodleBib were free software and more user-friendly, but they offered only two style manuals: APA and MLA. Another disadvantage was that they did not support searching and importing bibliographic records from library catalogs or online databases. [15]

A review of literature in Thai showed that not much has been researched on this topic area. Three papers dealt with standard formats for creating bibliographic records that helped in the retrieval of bibliographies from OPAC. These papers were written by Intha [16]; Hanprab [17]; and Teng-Amnuay with his co-researchers. [18]

Two papers were found to focus on bibliographic management area. In 1997, Wilairatanaporn studied and designed the reference database and bibliography constructor by using Coads object oriented analysis and design. He also analyzed the data structure and procedure of Word Chula version Chulacharuk 78 (Word processing software) and used Microsoft Visual C++ compiler to construct the program. Users could create or modify bibliographies in many styles. They could search and import or export data from databases. [19] In 1998, Tuamsuk and Sirichote compared the reference styles which were cited in the humanities and social sciences journals; and in the science and technology journals published in Thai language. Fourteen journals were selected for this study: seven titles in humanities and social sciences and the other seven in science and technology. They analyzed and compared "Rules/Instructions for Citations" of these journals. The findings showed different practices of in-text citing. In the humanities and social sciences journals, "Name-Year system or Harvard system" and "footnote" in-text citations were adopted. In the science and technology journals, "Alphabet-Number system" was preferable. However, in listing citations in the references for both groups of journals, citations were arranged by alphabetical order, beginning with citations of Thai language materials and following by those of English language materials. [20]

METHODOLOGY

In the present study, the SWU style manual was used to create templates of citation style of different types of materials by using EndNote version 9.0. The accuracy of the citation style was verified by checking with the SWU style manual. Then a one-page questionnaire was sent to 80 Thai academic libraries to collect Z39.50 configuration data. The data obtained was used to create Z39.50 connection files in EndNote program. The Z39.50 connection files created were tested by connecting, searching, and importing bibliographic records (in Thai and English language) from academic library catalogs. The accuracy and completeness of imported records were thoroughly examined.

Five scholars from various fields were invited to try out EndNote for managing their bibliography according to the SWU style manual. They were also asked to search, retrieve and import the bibliographic record from other academic libraries via the Z39.50 connection created. The try-outs provided useful comments and suggestions which were used to improve the bibliography templates and the connection files. In addition, 40 graduate students, who attended EndNote training session, were asked to give comments and suggestions for project improvement.

RESULTS

Research results were presented by two topics: the SWU style manual and Z39.50 connection to the academic library catalogs in Thailand.

SWU Style Manual

In analyzing the SWU style manual, it was found that EndNote could accommodate the construction of bibliography templates for 12 reference types as shown in Table 1.

Table 1. Description of Reference Types in SWU Style Manual

	Reference Types	Description
1.	Audiovisual Material	Audiovisual materials, unpublished work
2.	Book	Books in printed form and E-Book
3.	Book Section	Chapters and articles in various types of printed books such as textbook, encyclopedia,
4.	Edited Book	Translated books
5.	Electronic Article	Articles in E-Journal and E-Newspaper
6.	Electronic Source	Website, Webpage and Homepage
7.	Film or Broadcast	Radio and television programs
8.	Journal Article	Journal Articles in printed form
9.	Legal Rule or Regulation	Government gazetteer
10.	Newspaper Article	Newspaper articles in printed form
11.	Personal Communication	Interviews
12.	Thesis	Thesis, Dissertation, or Master's project in printed and electronic forms

A template of bibliographic structure was created for each reference type according to the SWU style manual as shown in Table 2.

Table 2. Structure of SWU Style Manual by Reference Types

Reference Types	Structure of SWU Style Manual
Audiovisual Material	Author.| (Year).| *Title.*| (Type).| City|: Publisher.
Book	Author.| (Year).| *Title.*| Edition.| City|: Publisher.| Accessed,| URL
Book Section	Author.| (Year).| Title.| In| *Book Title.*| Editor|. Volume.| Pages.| Edition.| City|: Publisher.
Edited Book	Author.| (Year).| *Title.*| Translator.| Edition.| City|: Publisher.
Electronic Article	Author.| (Year).| |Title.| *Periodical Title.*| Volume(Issue):| Pages.| Date Accessed,| URL
Electronic Source	Author.| (Year).| *Title.*| Edition.| City|: Publisher.| Access Date,| URL
Film or Broadcast	Director.| (Year Released).| Title.| *Series Title.*| Distributor.| Running Time.
Journal Article	Author.| (Year).| Title.| *Journal.*| Volume(Issue):| Pages.
Legal Rule or Regulation	Secondary Title.| (Year).| *Title.*| Rule Number| Section Number.| Pages.
Newspaper Article	Reporter.| (Year).| Title.| *Newspaper.*| Pages.
Personal Communication	Author.| (Year).| Recipient| Publisher.
Thesis	Author.| (Year).| *Title.*| Thesis Type.| City|: University.| Research Notes.| Access Date,| URL

However, to deal with language problem, it was necessary to create separate bibliography templates for "SWU Thai style manual" and "SWU English style manual." SWU Thai style manual was used for Thai language materials and SWU English style manual was used for English language materials.

Entering bibliographical data in Thai style manual was different from the English style manual as follows:

[1] Author name: The format for entering author names was *first name*, followed by space and *last name.*

[2] Edition: Edition needed to be entered in full no abbreviation was allowed.

[3] Date of access: The format of entering date was *date*, followed by space and *month* space and *year*.

Due to the complication of Thai language, EndNote could not arrange citations in a bibliography in alphabetical order perfectly. It could not recognize *title* in citations. Imported citations therefore needed to be edited. However, the ability to access and download / import citations outweighed the limitations described.

Z39.50 Connection to the Academic Library Catalogs in Thailand

In examining Z39.50 connection to the academic library catalogs in Thailand in 80 academic Thai libraries, findings (Table 3) were described in four categories:

(1) 13 libraries (16.25 percent) could be connected through Z39.50 connection in EndNote program. Bibliographic records both in Thai and English could be accessed and downloaded.
(2) In five libraries (6.25 percent), only bibliographic records in English could be searched and downloaded.
(3) The figure of libraries that were not yet ready to open Z39.50 searching service through EndNote was 25 (31.25 percent).
(4) There were 20 libraries (25 percent) which could not be connected via Z39.50 in EndNote.

Table 3. Situation on Z39.50 Connection of the Academic Libraries in Thailand

Situation	Libraries of Public Universities	Libraries of Rajamangala Universities of Technology	Libraries of Rajabhat Universities	Total	
				Number	Percent age
Search and download in Thai and English	10	-	3	13	16.25

Table 3. Continued

Situation	Libraries of Public Universities	Libraries of Rajamangala Universities of Technology	Libraries of Rajabhat Universities	Total	
				Number	Percent age
Search and download only in English	4	-	1	5	6.25
Unavailable service	7	5	13	25	31.25
Cannot be connected	5	2	13	20	25
Connection data are incomplete	5	2	10	17	21.25
Total	31	9	40	80	100

Z39.50 connection files of libraries in categories 1 and 2 were created as listed in Table 4 and 5.

Table 4. Z39.50 Connection Files of Academic Libraries in Thailand (Search and Download in Thai and English)

	Library Name	Connection Files
1.	Bansomdej Chaopraya Rajabhat University, Academic Resource Center & Information Technology	BSRU
2.	Buriram Rajabhat University, Academic Resource Center & Information Technology	BRU

3.	Khon Kaen University, Instructional Resources Centre	KKU
	Library Name	Connection Files
4.	Mae Fah Luang University, the Learning Resources and Education Media Center	MFU
5.	Mahachulalongkorn Rajwittayalai University, Central Library	MCU
6.	National Institute of Development Administration (NIDA), Library and Information Centre	NIDA_Book NIDA_Article
7.	Sakon Nakhon Rajabhat University, Academic Resource Center & Information Technology	SNRU
8.	Srinakharinwirot University, Central Library	SWUP
9.	Srinakharinwirot University, Ongkharak Library	SWUO
10.	Sukhothai Thammatirat Open University, Office of Documentation and Information	STOU
11.	Suranaree University of Technology, The Centre for Library Resources and Educational Media	SUT
12.	Taksin University Library	TSU
13.	Thammasat University Library	TU_Book TU_Article

It was found that most library catalogs used Buddhist era for Thai materials in Tag 008 of MARC records. The EndNote did not recognize Buddhist era, so the system could not retrieve the publication date. As such, all bibliographic data fields could be imported, except for "year." Only two library catalogs used Christian era for Thai materials, they were the library catalogs of Sukhothai Thammatirat Open University and Mahachulalongkorn Rajwittayalai University.

Table 5. Z39.50 Connection Files of Academic Libraries in Thailand (Search and Download only in English)

	Library Name	Connection Files
1.	Kasetsart University, Main Library	KU
2.	King Mongkut's Institute of Technology, Chaokhun Taharn Lan Krabang, Central Library	KMITL
3.	King Mongkut's University of Technology, Thonburi, Library and Documentation Centre	KMUTT
4.	Ramkhamhaeng University Library	RU
5.	Thepastri Rajabhat University, Academic Resource Center & Information Technology	TRU

The connection files were created from Z39.50 connection configuration of academic libraries in categories 1 and 2 as shown in Table 6.

Table 6. Z39.50 Connection Configuration of Academic Libraries in Thailand

Library Name	System Name	Server	Server Address	Database	Database Name	Port ID
BRU	VTLS	Sunfire 210	opac.bru.ac.th	vtls01	default	1111
BSRU	VTLS	Book.bsru.ac.th	Book.bsru.ac.th	vtls	default	1111
KKU	Innopac	kkulib.kku.ac.th	kkulib.kku.ac.th	innopac	innopac	210
KMITL	Innopac	161.246.37.11	161.246.37.11	innopac	innopac	210
KMUTT	Innopac	kmittlib.lib.kmutt.ac .th	kmittlib.lib.kmutt. ac .th	innopac	innopac	210

Table 6. (Continued)

Library Name	System Name	Server	Server Address	Database	Database Name	Port ID
KU	Innopac	158.108.80.5	158.108.80.5	innopac	innopac	210
MCU	VTLS	Sun Fire V240	vtls.mcu.ac.th	vtls01	default	1111
MFU	VTLS	lib.mfu.ac.th	lib.mfu.ac.th	vtls	default	1111
NIDA	Horizon (Book)	202.28.16.20	202.28.16.20	horizon	nida	210
	Horizon (Thai Journal Index)	library1.nida.ac.th	library1.nida.ac.th	horizon	nida	210
RU	Innopac	library.lib.ru.ac.th	library.lib.ru.ac.th	innopac	innopac	210
SNRU	VTLS	202.29.24.61	202.29.24.61	clas01	default	1111
STOU	VTLS	202.28.103.52	202.28.103.52	vtls	default	1111
SUT	Horizon	203.158.6.4	203.158.6.4	horizon	hzndb	210
SWUO	Horizon	Okdb	10.2.17.4	horizon	hzndb	210
SWUP	Horizon	lib.swu.ac.th	library.swu.ac.th	horizon	hzndb	210
TRU	Horizon	library.tru.ac.th	library.tru.ac.th	horizon	hzndb	210
TSU	Horizon	lib.tsu.ac.th	lib.tsu.ac.th	horizon	hzndb	210
TU	Horizon (Book)	search.library.tu.ac.th	search.library.tu.ac .th	horizon	hzndb	210
	Horizon (Thai Journal Index)	index.library.tu.ac.th	index.library.tu.ac. th	horizon	hzndb	210

In the cataloging module, most Thai academic libraries created journal index for Thai articles. The cataloging databases of some libraries contained both material catalogs and journal index, for instance, Khon Kaen University Library, Ongkharak Library and the Central Library of Srinakharinwirot University. In other libraries, catalog database and index database were maintained separately. These libraries included Thammasat University Library and the Library of the National Institute of Development Administration (NIDA). In both cases, library patrons could search and download bibliographic records, but the imported data was not in the right format; for example, *journal title* will appear in *note field.* So the imported data needed to be arranged according to the standard format. The same problem occurred in downloading bibliographic records of theses and dissertations from the cataloging databases because EndNote software was not perfectly compatible with the cataloging module software.

The abbreviations of names of Thai academic libraries were spelt out in Table 7.

Table 7. Full Name of Thai Academic Libraries

Abbreviation	Full Name
BRU	Buriram Rajabhat University, Academic Resource Center & Information Technology, Buriram Province
BSRU	Bansomdej Chaopraya Rajabhat University, Academic Resource Center & Information Technology, Bangkok
KKU	Khon Kaen University, Instructional Resources Centre, Khon Kaen Province
KMITL	King Mongkut's Institute of Technology, Chaokhun Taharn Lan Krabang, Central Library, Bangkok
KMUTT	King Mongkut's University of Technology, Thonburi, Library and Documentation Centre, Bangkok
KU	Kasetsart University, Main Library, Bangkok
MC	Mahachulalongkorn Rajwittayalai University, Central Library, Bangkok
MFU	Mae Fah Luang University, the Learning Resources and Education Media Center, Chaingrai Province
NIDA	National Institute of Development Administration (NIDA), Library and Information Centre, Bangkok
RU	Ramkhamhaeng University Library, Bangkok

Table 7. Continued

Abbreviation	Full Name
SNRU	Sakon Nakhon Rajabhat University, Academic Resource Center & Information Technology, Sakon Nakhon Province
STOU	Sukhothai Thammatirat Open University, Office of Documentation and Information, Nonthaburi Province
SUT	Suranaree University of Technology, The Centre for Library Resources and Educational Media, Nakhon Ratchasima Province
SWUO	Srinakharinwirot University, Ongkharak Library, Nakhonnayok Province
SWUP	Srinakharinwirot University, Central Library, Bangkok
TRU	Thepastri Rajabhat University, Academic Resource Center & Information Technology, Lopburi Province
TSU	Taksin University Library, Songkla Province
TU	Thammasat University Library, Bangkok

Discussion and Conclusion

In Thailand, many students lack skills in creating bibliographies. Thus, instruction of how to use EndNote program should be helpful and increase the accuracy and consistency of citations. The program is user-friendly to students because they can import bibliographical data and do the tasks of alphabetization and punctuation automatically. However, in order to be able to cite properly and create bibliography, students need to understand various parts of a book and other information materials, for example; author, title, place, publisher, date of publication, etc.

EndNote or any bibliographic management software is not popular in Thailand. Most students have hardly heard of it. There are only a small group of scholars in Science and Health Science who know about it and use it. One reason for low use of software including EndNote is that they are not quite affordable. So the universities should provide EndNote or any other bibliographic management software for use in libraries, computer laboratories, and graduate schools. In addition, management of bibliography should be integrated in such courses as research methodology and information literacy skills. In the meantime,

Thai academic libraries should be the leader in promoting the application of the software by organizing training courses for library patrons.

As mention earlier, the library collections in Thai universities consist of both Thai and English materials. Thai language materials are more difficult and costly to be organized in an automated system, especially indexing. There are only 13 library catalog systems which can be searched in Thai language via Z39.50 connection of EndNote program. Thai language is a major barrier in developing Z39.50 searching connection of bibliographic management software. Some libraries are at the beginning stage of automation and are not ready to open Z39.50 searching service. Some are not aware of the advantages of Z39.50 connection. Others wrongly assume that Z39.50 configuration needs to be kept confidential for system security purpose. They close the access port or protect it with firewall. Library patrons, therefore, cannot connect, search or download needed information.

On a positive note, Thai academic Libraries have participated in cooperative cataloguing in order to avoid duplicating cataloguing activities and to share resources. The cooperation has resulted in the Union Catalog, a shared resource for all universities in Thailand that can be conveniently accessible by library patrons. At present, the Union Catalog's working group is studying MARC details in order to establish the same standard. [21] This project requires the application of Z39.50 standard for resource sharing. The patrons will certainly benefit more, should all academic libraries agree to develop Z39.50 connection for Thai Language materials and promote Z39.50 standard in bibliographic management program.

REFERENCES

[1.] *Citing your sources: what is plagiarism?* (2007). Retrieved September 11, 2007, from http://www.lib.berkeley.edu/instruct/guides/citations.html

[2.] Wareesa-ard, A. (2008). *Use of the EndNote program for bibliographic management in Srinakharinwirot University's style*. Bangkok, Thailand: Faculty of Humanities, Srinakharinwirot University.

[3.] Bhakdibutr, C., & Keesiri, S. (1999). *University libraries in Thailand*. Retrieved September 9, 2007, from http://tla.tiac.or.th/ifla/Ifla99_6.htm

[4.] Wareesa-ard, A. (2004, November). The role of academic libraries in developing library automation network in Thailand. *The Journal of Academic Librarianship, 30*(6), 502-506.

[5.] *Bibliography software: your guide to bibliography software on the web.* (2007).Retrieved October 4, 2007, from http://www.educational-software-directory.net/
reference/bibliography.html

[6.] *Thomson ResearchSoft: products.* (2007). Retrieved October 9, 2007, from http://thomsonresearchsoft.com/products

[7.] Evans, P. (2007). *Personal bibliographic managers: personal research assistants.* Retrieved October 1, 2007, from http://www.bibliotech.com/html/PBMS.html

[8.] *Z39.50 questions & answers.* (2007). Retrieved October 1, 2007, from http://www.libraryhq.com/z3950qa.html

[9.] Kunin, C. M. (1985). Managing bibliographic citations using microcomputers. *The American Journal of Medicine, 78*(4), 627-634.

[10.] Sato, H., Sato, S., & Horikoshi, I. (1996). Implementation of a reference management system, MacRefer, under HyperCard [On-line serial]. Computer Methods and Programs in Biomedicine, 50, 53-61. Retrieved September 3, 2007 from http://www.sciencedirect.com/science/article/B6T5J-3W0NGTR-6/2/62b923402242a00ddb8d32ba71d80939

[11.] East, J. W. (2003). Z39.50 and personal bibliographic software. *Library Hi Tech*, 21, 34-43.

[12.] Krooden, E. T. (2004). Teaching information literacy courses in Southern Africa: lessons learned in training on constructing personal bibliographic databases [On-line serial]. *Journal of Education for Library and Information Science*, 45, 221-228. Retrieved September 3, 2007 from http://vnweb.hwwilsonweb.com/hww/jumpstart.
jhtml?recid=bc05f7a67b1790e57592a52cf289f6ee30c4e752ce8c1e6e5c785
cbde3148ce131ef6fc9eb3954d&fmt=C

[13.] Gall, C., & Brahmi, F. A. (2004). Retrieval comparison of EndNote to search MEDLINE (Ovid and PubMed) versus searching them directly. *Medical Reference Services Quarterly*, 23, 25-32.

[14.] McGeachin, R. B. (2004). The impact of electronic bibliographic databases and electronic journal articles on the scholar's information-seeking behavior and personal collection of "reprints" [On-line serial]. *Science & Technology Libraries*, 25, 127-137. Retrieved September 3, 2007 from http://vnweb.hwwilsonweb.com/hww/jumpstart.jht
ml?recid=0bc05f7a67b1790e57592a52cf289f6ee30c4e752ce8c1e6d78cb74
277dfb6d43eeb314859742e84&fmt=C

[15.] Kessler, J., & Van Ullen, M. K. (2005). Citation generators: generating bibliographies for the next generation. *The Journal of Academic Librarianship*, 31, 310-316.

[16.] Intha, W. (2001). *A cataloging format of internet resources for government universities.* Chiang Mai, Thailand: Graduate School, Chiang Mai University.

[17.] Harnprab, P. (2003). *A study of the accuracy of MARC records of books in Thai.* Bangkok, Thailand: Graduate School, Srinakharinwirot University.

[18.] Teng-amnuay, Y., Chaithammapakorn, S., & Sutaveepramochanon, N. (2002). *Design and specification of bibliographical record format and storage procedure for preservation of chunked continuous data stream for retrieval through library automation: a case study on internet traffic statistics of Chulalongkorn University.* Bangkok, Thailand: Chulalongkorn University.

[19.] Wilairatanaporn, C. (1997). *Reference database and bibliography constructor.* Bangkok, Thailand: Graduate School, Chulalongkorn University.

[20.] Tuamsuk, K., & Sirichote, P. (1998). *A comparative study of reference styles in humanities and social sciences journals and science and technology journals printed in Thai language.* Khon Kaen, Thailand: Faculty of Humanities and Social Sciences, Khon Kaen University.

[21.] Wareesa-ard, A. (2004, November). *loc.cit.*

Reviewed By

Dr. Aree Cheunwattana, Lecturer in Library & Information Science Faculty of Humanities Srinakharinwirot University Bangkok, Thailand Tel. 662-6495552 Fax: 662-2600122 *Email: areech@swu.ac.th*

In: Academic Librarianship in the 21st Century ISBN: 978-1-60456-865-3
Editors: C. M.Garcia and T. A.Flores

Chapter 4

FAIR USE IN THE TWENTY-FIRST CENTURY: A LIBRARIAN'S PERSPECTIVE

Angela Weiler
Coulter Library, Onondaga Community College, Syracuse, New York, USA

ABSTRACT

In recent years, the Fair Use doctrine of United States copyright law has been continually tested in the courts. Recently a Judge Alex Kozinski of the 9th U.S. Circuit Court of Appeals went so far as to call fair use a "red herring" and declared that "we should just dump it" (Kozinski & Newman, 1999).

Librarians have been championing the fair use rights of the American public since long before those rights were actually codified by copyright law. However, more recently many librarians and other educators have been hesitant to use certain materials in an educational setting, fearful of attracting the notice of litigious publishers, recording companies, and other content owners. Campuses' legal representation have only increased this feeling of malaise, taking a "better safe than sorry" stance on fair use of intellectual property.

It is difficult to predict the effect that proposed legislation such as the "Intellectual Property Rights Enforcement Act" or the "Curb Illegal Downloading on College Campuses Act of 2007" may have on campuses and libraries; future court cases will also have a large impact on fair use rights as they have been historically exercised. It can be surmised that the cautionary atmosphere already created by the Digital Millennium Copyright Act and other recent legislation will only increase, creating an even more inhibitive environment with regard to educational use of intellectual property.

This chapter will provide an overview of current trends, legislation, and litigation related to fair use of intellectual property as it impacts academic libraries in the United States. It will explore recent developments in fair use issues such as scholarly publishing and library electronic reserves, and give examples of initiatives currently being used on campuses to retain, secure, and exercise fair use rights in the twenty-first century.

INTRODUCTION

Librarians have been champions of the fair use rights of the American public since well before those rights were actually codified by section 107 of federal copyright law. However, in recent years many librarians and other educators have been increasingly hesitant to use materials in an educational setting, fearful of attracting the notice of litigious publishers, media companies, and other content owners. Campuses' legal representation have only increased this feeling of malaise, taking a "better safe than sorry" stance on fair use of intellectual property.

Since 1976, librarians have been for the most part relying on any one of a number of "guidelines" in making decisions regarding patron use of material for educational purposes, particularly as related to course reserves materials. However, due to a combination of factors, these guidelines can end up restricting patron access even more than the law requires. Librarians also turn to section 108 of copyright law (Limitations to Exclusive Rights: Libraries and Archives) for guidance in copyright issues. However, in order to be able to make fully informed decisions on copyright issues without needlessly restricting patron access, librarians should consider using section 107, the fair use doctrine, in making their final determination.

BACKGROUND

Most librarians are at least somewhat familiar with the history of United States copyright law, beginning with Article I, Section 8 of the U.S. Constitution:

> " The Congress shall have power … To promote the Progress of Science and useful Arts, by securing for limited Times to Authors and

> Inventors the exclusive Right to their respective Writings and Discoveries …" (U.S. House of Representatives, 2004)

The language of Section 8 mentions three areas: promoting learning ("the Progress of Science and useful Arts"); preserving the public domain ("securing for limited Times"); and benefiting creators of work ("the exclusive Right to their respective Writings and Discoveries") (Patterson & Lindberg, 1991). Legislation and court decisions have regularly cited this constitutional mandate when deciding copyright cases. Some examples:

> "Congress must weigh the public costs and benefits derived from protecting a particular interest. "The constitutional purpose of copyright is to facilitate the flow of ideas in the interest of learning."...The primary objective of our copyright laws is not to reward the author, but rather to secure for the public the benefits from the creations of authors."
>
> *Berne Convention Implementation Act of 1988*

> "The primary objective of copyright is not to reward the labor of authors, but "to promote the Progress of Science and useful Arts."
>
> *Justice Sandra Day O'Connor*
> *Feist Publications, Inc. v. Rural Telephone Service*

> "From the infancy of copyright protection, some opportunity for fair use of copyrighted materials has been thought necessary to fulfill copyright's very purpose, "[t]o promote the Progress of Science and useful Arts . . . ."
>
> *Justice David H. Souter*
> *Luther R. Campbell Aka Luke Skyywalker, et al., Petitioners V. Acuff Rose Music*

> "[The Supreme Court has] often recognized the monopoly privileges that Congress has authorized, while "intended to motivate the creative activity of authors and inventors by the provision of a special reward," are limited in nature and must ultimately serve the public good."
>
> *Chief Justice Rehnquist*
> *John C. Fogerty, Petitioner V. Fantasy, Inc.*

As we proceed with this chapter, it is important to remember Section 8 of the United States Constitution, as it lays out very simply and clearly the original purpose and spirit of copyright law in the United States, and is consistently reaffirmed by the courts in deciding copyright issues.

GUIDELINES BACKGROUND

The most recent major revision of Title 17 was the Copyright Act of 1976, which for the first time codified the doctrine of fair use (to be discussed later in this chapter). At that time, the Senate Judiciary Committee's recommended that "representatives of authors, book and periodical publishers and other owners of copyrighted material" meet to come up with guidelines in order to help libraries determine under what conditions work could be copied, displayed, distributed, etc. under the new law. Their desire was that the committee help libraries to, among other things, distinguish between "single copies" and "systematic reproduction" (Heller, 2004).

In response to this recommendation, the Commission on Technological Uses of Copyrighted Works (CONTU) was formed, consisting of three groups: the Ad Hoc Committee on Copyright Law Revision, the Association of American Publishers, and the Authors League of America. (The Ad Hoc Committee on Copyright Law Revision represented educational interests, and was comprised of representatives of thirty-nine separate educational groups.) This commission worked to develop an agreement detailing exactly how much material the content owners would consent to being used by educators and libraries without their having to ask permission (i.e., exactly how much, in their opinion, constituted a "fair use").

The CONTU addressed their attentions to two new sections of Title 17 - Copyright: Section 107 – Fair Use, and Section 108 – Libraries. The language addressing classroom use occurs in section 107, whereas section 108 was written specifically for libraries. Section 108 clearly states that it does not affect libraries' rights of fair use in any way, which means that libraries are always free to refer back to the four points of fair use when contemplating whether or not to use materials. Section 108 does not address works of music, so those guidelines are included under the section 107 guidelines on fair use (Kranich, 1984).

The commission developed a comprehensive set of guidelines called "The Agreement on Guidelines for Classroom Copying in Not-For-Profit Educational Institutions With Respect To Books And Periodicals". These guidelines attach specific quantities to clarify the concept of brevity and spontaneity as applied to various types of intellectual property. For example, educators were allowed to make copies of ("(II)(a) A complete poem if less than 250 words and if printed on not more than two pages or, (b) from a longer poem, an excerpt of not more than 250 words" for classroom use (United States Copyright Office, 1995).

This agreement has been widely used by libraries ever since. The first sentence of these guidelines, agreed upon by all parties, clearly states that they represent "*the minimum and not the maximum* standards of educational fair use" [emphasis mine]. The parties also agreed that "There may be instances in which copying which does not fall within the guidelines stated below may nonetheless be permitted under the criteria of fair use." (United States Copyright Office, 1995).

These two clarifications are often forgotten or ignored in contemporary library policies. All too often libraries cite these percentages, numbers of words, or number of pages as being the maximum amounts patrons can use (Hoffman, 2005).

PROBLEMS WITH GUIDELINES

The CONTU guidelines have not changed since they were drawn up in 1976. However, copyright law has indeed changed, and thirty years of case law has set new precedents and offered differing interpretations of copyright law in general, and fair use in particular. In addition, there have been a number of statutes passed since 1976 which have changed copyright law in several areas. While the more controversial areas of these laws are well known to librarians, some also contain provisions that were meant to safeguard areas of education and research, libraries, and archives. One must look at these recent changes, as well as case law and Title 17 itself, to accurately determine the current state of copyright as it pertains to educational institutions.

Since 1976, a number of other guidelines on copyright issues in libraries have been developed to interpret the many areas of copyright law which contain non-specific language such as "small portion" and "limited number". These sets of guidelines list the percentages of works and the exact numbers of chapters, articles, words, etc. which can be used by a library without fear of litigation. They have been developed by librarians, attorneys, and content owners, and they represent educated opinions and interpretations of copyright law; but the guidelines themselves are not law. Indeed, a comparison of guidelines from various sources reveals that their interpretation of the law differs somewhat, depending on their provenance. Guidelines notwithstanding, the courts have sometimes determined uses of material in commercial ventures to be fair, even when that use exceeds the amount recommended in the guidelines for educational use. In fact, for the most part, these guidelines are neither mentioned, nor adhered to, by the courts in rendering their decisions (Gould, Lipinski and Buchanan, 2005).

COPYRIGHT CLEARANCE CENTER

In addition to helping with the development of guidelines, the publishing industry took their own steps to protect their interests. In 1978 the Copyright Clearance Center was formed to facilitate seeking, and paying for, permission to use intellectual property. The CCC is not a government entity, but is rather a non-profit organization set up by publishers, and "each year [they] return tens of millions of dollars in royalties to U.S. rights holders" (Copyright Clearance Center International Licensing and Permissions, 2007). An increasing portion of these millions of dollars come from colleges and universities, who ask for permission to use a work and then allow the Copyright Clearance Center to determine whether their use of a work is a fair one or not.

At about the same time that the Copyright Clearance Center was formed, the Association of American Publishers and the Author's League of America issued a set of their own guidelines for photocopying which stated that libraries could copy *only* under the provisions of section 108 of copyright law [Sec. 108. Limitations on exclusive rights: Reproduction by libraries and archives] (Heller, 2004). This is, of course, not true: Section 108 clearly states that "nothing in this section in any way affects the right of fair use as provided by section 107" (United States Copyright Office, 2003).

The CCC's stance is that "fair use is not an exception to copyright compliance so much as it is a "legal defense"(Copyright Clearance Center, 2007), a definition which seems to change depending on which side of the fair use issue one is on. The law itself calls fair use one of several "limitations to exclusive rights", and section 108 actually refers to "the right of fair use". Yet publishers who work with the CCC receive standard notice templates to place in their publications which state that libraries must contact the CCC and pay the stated fee to use the work in any way. There is no mention of fair use in these notices (Patterson and Lindberg, 1991).

It is entirely possible that, in relying on the publishing industry's interpretations of copyright law, colleges and universities have paid unnecessary fees to the CCC. In addition, librarians themselves may have been enforcing guidelines that are far more restrictive and rigid than necessary in an effort to steer clear of litigation, or on the advice of campus legal counsel (Gould et al, 2005).

Section 107, however, can be applied by anyone, including libraries, who can prove the four points of fair use. A well-constructed, educated evaluation and application of the fair use exemption to exclusive rights can always be argued, regardless of existing "guidelines". If one prefers some type of linear guide in determining uses of materials, the "Fair Use Checklist", developed by Copyright

Management Center of Indiana University and available at <http://www.copyright.iupui.edu/checklist.pdf> is an example of a less rigid, more balanced approach to weighing fair use. The checklist provides prompts for each of the four points of fair use which enable an individual to give thoughtful consideration to those points themselves before making a decision.

FAIR USE BACKGROUND

The concept of fair use first appeared in England, although it was not then widely used (Hoffman, 2005). In the United States, fair use began as a doctrine, developing over a period of years from case law. The concept was first mentioned in a Supreme Court decision handed down by Judge William Story in 1841 regarding use of the letters of George Washington in a work written about his life. Judge Story stated "that a fair and bona fide abridgement of an original work, is not a piracy of the copyright of the author." He also set out the following points to be examined when deciding copyright cases: "the nature and objects of the selections made, the quantity and value of the materials used, and the degree in which the use may prejudice the sale, or diminish the profits, or supersede the objects, of the original work." (Folsom v. Marsh, 1841). This decision formed the foundation of the fair use doctrine.

In 1935, a "Gentleman's' Agreement" between publishers and libraries was drawn up regarding copying for scholarly research, establishing the custom of allowing a single reproduction of copyrighted material by a scholar, "solely for the purposes of research." In part because of this "custom", the case of *Williams & Wilkins v. The United States* was decided in 1972 in favor of the National Library of Medicine's right to copy materials from medical journals and distribute them via interlibrary loan for educational purposes.

Williams & Wilkins was the first case to decide that modern, large scale photocopying by libraries for scholarship and research is a fair use; indeed, publishers were so shaken by this decision that then-chairman of the Copyright Committee of the Association of American Publishers organized a fund to take the case to the Supreme Court. The case was accepted, but eventually ended in a 4 – 4 split decision (with one justice not taking part). This left the lower court decision standing, and freed libraries to photocopy materials for research and scholarship (Goldstein, 2003).

In 1976, the Copyright Act was ratified, passing the fair use doctrine into statutory form for the first time. Since then, the fair use statute has been continually tested in the courts.

The actual text of Section 107 is brief:

> Sec. 107. Limitations on exclusive rights: Fair use Notwithstanding the provisions of sections 106 and 106A, the fair use of a copyrighted work, including such use by reproduction in copies or phonorecords or by any other means specified by that section, for purposes such as criticism, comment, news reporting, teaching (including multiple copies for classroom use), scholarship, or research, is not an infringement of copyright. In determining whether the use made of a work in any particular case is a fair use the factors to be considered shall include
>
> [1] the purpose and character of the use, including whether such use is of a commercial nature or is for nonprofit educational purposes;
>
> [2] the nature of the copyrighted work;
>
> [3] the amount and substantiality of the portion used in relation to the copyrighted work as a whole; and
>
> [4] the effect of the use upon the potential market for or value of the copyrighted work.
>
> The fact that a work is unpublished shall not itself bar a finding of fair use if such finding is made upon consideration of all the above factors (United States Copyright Office, 2003).

None of these four points supersedes any of the others in importance; each is, in theory, considered equally by the courts. However, because almost all more recent court decisions on copyright issues have involved for-profit corporations as opposed to non-profit entities, it would be reasonable to assume that "the effect of the use upon the potential market for or value of the copyrighted work" has been a central issue in these cases (Dames, 2005).

In 1997, the Conference on Fair Use was convened to open up discussions on fair use issues in consideration of technological developments. Electronic reserves was one of a number of issues discussed, but participants were unable to come to an agreement. Regardless of the lack of consensus, guidelines were indeed issued, but many library organizations do not condone their use because they are considered to be too restrictive. Nevertheless, some colleges and universities have still chosen to use them (Albanese, 2005), (Waldman, Goldberg, and Heins, 2005).

Fair use has become such a controversial area that a 9th U.S. Circuit Court of Appeals judge called it a "red herring" and declared that "we should just dump it" (Kozinski & Newman, 1999). Although librarians may not agree with his suggestion, those feelings of frustration certainly exist, in the private sector as well as in academe, in trying to sort out fair use issues on campuses and in libraries.

Recent Legal Developments

Several laws related to copyright have been passed in the past ten years or so, and three of them are particularly well-known to librarians: the Digital Millennium Copyright Act of 1998 (the "DMCA"); the Copyright Term Extension Act of 1999 (also known as the "Sonny Bono Act" or the "Mickey Mouse Act"); and The Technology, Education, and Copyright Harmonization Act of 2002 (also known as the TEACH Act). All of these have implications for libraries, both positive and negative.

Digital Millennium Copyright Act (1998)

As most librarians are already aware, the Digital Millennium Copyright Act contains several areas which directly impact libraries. It lays out specific conditions which must be implemented by educational institutions regarding network systems in order for those institutions to continue to provide materials for scholarship and research. Online-service providers (including educational institutions) are given protection against liability if they follow certain procedures such as designating a campus "copyright agent" to track claims of infringement; adopting an official campus copyright policy; and disabling access to materials should the institution become aware of "claimed infringement".

When in doubt about how the DMCA impacts a use, librarians are well-advised to remember one important clause in that law. As with Title 17 - section 108, the DMCA also clearly states that "Nothing in this section shall affect rights, remedies, limitations, or defenses to copyright infringement, including fair use, under this title" (Public Law No. 105-304).

Copyright Term Extension Act (1999)

The public domain was established by the U.S. Constitution when it referred to the "limited times" that rights are granted to creators/owners in order to encourage them to create new work. After that limited time period elapses, intellectual property passes into the public domain, where it exists in perpetuity for the benefit of "science and the useful arts".

The original Copyright Act of 1790 ("An Act for the Encouragement of Learning") stipulated a 14 year copyright term, renewable once for another 14 years if the author was still living. Over a hundred years later, the 1909 copyright act doubled that number, to two 28 year terms. In 1976 the term of copyright changed to the life of the author plus 50 years, this time more than doubling the term in most cases.

Most recently, the Copyright Term Extension Act of 1998 (the "Sonny Bono Act") added another twenty years to the duration of copyright, both for authors and for corporate works, anonymous works, and works for hire. The act is also sometimes called the "Mickey Mouse Act" because the Mickey Mouse cartoon character was about to pass into the public domain when the act was drafted, and many perceived the law to have been drafted primarily to prevent that from happening. The following statement made by Congresswoman Mary Bono on October 07, 1998 (who succeeded her husband in the House of Representatives), speaks to the rationale behind more recent efforts to extend the duration of copyright:

> " ... Sonny wanted the term of copyright protection to last forever. I am informed by staff that such a change would violate the Constitution. ... As you know, there is also Jack Valenti's [president of the Motion Picture Association of America] proposal for [copyright] term to last forever less one day. Perhaps the Committee may look at that next Congress." (Bono, 1998).

Educators and libraries argued against passage of the Copyright Term Extension Act, which they believed would further limit the public domain and public access to intellectual property, stifling creativity and research. They also argued that the more dated portion the body of intellectual property affected would likely not be lucrative to its owners, having outlived its popularity, but would nonetheless remain inaccessible to the public, thus serving no useful purpose to anyone. (Hoffman, 2005).

To address these concerns, a provision was added to the act which allows libraries and archives, during the last 20 years of a copyright term, "to reproduce, distribute, display, or perform in facsimile or digital form a copy ... for purposes of preservation, scholarship, or research, if such library or archives has first determined, on the basis of reasonable investigation ... "that the work not "subject to normal commercial exploitation" or that a copy of the work cannot be "obtained at a reasonable price" (Public Law No. 1055-298).

Teach Act (2002)

The Technology, Education, and Copyright Harmonization Act of 2002 changed Title 17 to address distance education, changes which are found primarily in section 110(2). It lays out conditions whereby qualified educational institutions may use materials on web sites and in digital form in distance education. Those conditions have very specific requirements, and subsequently many campuses have added written copyright policies and designated a copyright "officer" who would be responsible for receiving claims of infringement as specified by the law.

The TEACH Act treats distance education as similar to traditional classroom education, in that materials are expected to be made available to students, used by students within a specific time period, and then are no longer available to the student. The Act does not permit copying/ scanning and/or uploading of entire works for students to refer to throughout the semester. The institution is responsible for restricting access to materials, for developing a copyright policy, and for disseminating copyright information to students and faculty. The good news is that the TEACH Act expanded the materials allowed, and now permits use of almost any kind of work The law also permits digitizing works, but only if the work is not already available in digital form. The materials made available to students, however, can only be made available "to the extent technologically feasible", and then only to those "students officially enrolled in the course". Also important: as long as the institution removes access to materials once students in a particular section of a course are finished, the institution can leave the materials on the system and "retrieve that content for future uses consistent with the new law" (Crews, 2002).

The TEACH Act was supported by libraries and educators, and addresses many issues that were uncertain prior to its passage. However, one noticeable omission in the act was that it did not address e-reserves at all.

None of these three acts, nor any other recent legislation, has rescinded or changed the language of section 107 Fair Use (Pike, 2006). In fact, despite Judge Kozinski's suggestion to "just dump it", fair use is not only still being used effectively in the courtroom, it has been upheld in a number of important recent decisions.

Perfect 10 V. Google

This case established the right of Google to search and post thumbnail images belonging to Perfect 10. The images, although password protected, are freely available on other web sites without the permission of Perfect 10. The final decision in this case was in Google's favor, relying heavily on a previous decision in a similar case dealing with thumbnail images (Kelly v. Arriba). The judge cited the "highly transformative" nature of Google's use of the images, as well as the "public benefit" derived from that use, reiterating once again the original purpose of copyright as stated in the Constitution. A noteworthy legal point in this case is that the court assigned Perfect 10 the responsibility for proving that Google did *not* have a fair use defense, rather than Google having to prove that it did (Pike, 2007).

Other Recent Developments: E-Reserves

Librarians often think of Basic Books v. Kinko's Graphics Corp. (1991) and other "course pack" cases when thinking of educational fair use. However, those cases involved publishers suing private companies such as Kinko's for reproducing and selling copyrighted materials. The fact that the use was educational did not override the fact that the course packs were being sold. The publishers' argument was that these course packs were supplanting sales, and thus adversely affecting the market for the works; both cases were decided not to be fair uses. These cases were decided against private firms, not educational institutions.

E-reserves, however, is turning out to be an area of growing concern to publishers, primarily because of the broad scale of the use and the digital nature of the information. When the Conference on Fair Use brought representatives of roughly ninety different interested parties together, e-reserves was one of the fair use issues they attempted to address. Perhaps as a consequence of CONFU's failure to find consensus on the topic, publishers have recently challenged a number of larger universities e-reserves policies.

In 2003 the Association of American Publishers contacted the University of California at San Diego and demanded that their library take "prompt action" to stop so-called "illegal reproduction, display, and distribution of copyrighted works." The AAP's representative stated that the publishers had "gotten glimpses" of some "detailed bibliographic information" from the UCSD library. The reason they had only "gotten glimpses" was that the e-reserves were password-protected so that only the appropriate students could access them.

The publishers' representative felt that that e-reserves were being used indiscriminately, substituting for purchased materials, and that UCSD's e-reserves was "tantamount to providing electronic course packs" (Albanese, 2005). Although no formal suit was filed, University of California attorneys stated that "when you allege infringement, you always raise the possibility of a lawsuit" (Albanese, 2007).

The Copyright Clearance Center guidelines state that electronic reserves are subject to the same rules that apply to print reserves; however, they also state that "E-reserves require the same permissions as course packs" (Copyright Clearance Center, 2007). This, again, is the publishers' interpretation of the law. The ACRL, on the other hand, has gone so far as to state that the "reserve room is an extension of the classroom", making multiple copies a permitted use under section 107 (Kranich, 1984).

Cornell University was contacted by the Association of American Publishers in April of 2006 regarding what it perceived to be "widespread copyright infringement" in their electronic reserve readings. Cornell responded by issuing "revised guidelines" for faculty as well as providing them with the "Checklist for Fair Use" from Indiana University. Cornell has since adopted its own Checklist for Fair Use", based on the Indiana model (Cornell University Copyright Information Center, 2007). The guidelines and checklist were distributed to Cornell faculty to increase their awareness of copyright and fair use issues; however, Cornell's existing library reserve policy remained the same. After the distribution of the materials in May of 2007, faculty reserve requests at Cornell dropped by seventy percent (Bridges, 2007).

In the past few years, publishers have also contacted, and reached agreements with, Syracuse, Marquette, and Hofstra universities. One university, however, did not respond to publishers' pressures to collaborate on copyright policy. As a result, the first bona fide lawsuit regarding academic fair use of copyrighted materials was brought against Georgia State University on April 15, 2008 by three publishers: Oxford University Press, Cambridge University Press, and SAGE

Publications. (The dean of libraries is personally named in the suit.) The suit cites “pervasive, flagrant, and ongoing unauthorized distribution of copyrighted materials” by way of the university’s course management systems, library e-reserves, and departmental web pages (Albanese, 2008). In their response to the suit, Georgia State contended that their practices are covered under the fair use statute (Hafner, 2008). This suit was brought after publishers’ attempts to talk with Georgia State regarding its copyright policies went unanswered; the lawsuit is currently still pending.

SOME CONSIDERATIONS

Licensing

Licenses are very important to libraries, because they articulate what the library may or may not do with any given material. Signing a database license can void any rights held by a library under any section in Title 17, including section 107 fair use (Heller, 2004). On the other hand, a database license may also grant uses of the content which the library might not normally have thought to be fair ones. The important point to remember is that every license should be read over carefully, by legal counsel if possible, before it is signed. In addition, any contract may be changed by either party, simply by writing in the change. All changes, however, must be initialed by both parties before the signed contract becomes valid.

Good Faith

All the reading and weighing and agonizing which librarians do over e-reserves and other fair use issues might arguably be seen as evidence of “good faith”. Title 17, section 504(2)(c) states that statutory damages for copyright infringement may be substantially reduced if the “infringer was not aware and had no reason to believe that his or her acts constituted infringement of copyright”, e.g., if they acted “in good faith” that their actions were lawful (Gould, et al, 2005). For instance, password-protection of e-reserves to limit access to only enrolled students might provide some evidence of a library acting in good faith to protect publisher’s interests.

Sovereign Immunity

A University of California representative stated that, although the Association of American Publishers might sue them, they could not collect monetary damages because states are protected constitutionally by sovereign immunity (Bridges, 2007). However, section 501 of Title 17 now states that anyone can be sued for infringement, and that "anyone includes any State, any instrumentality of a State, and any officer or employee of a state or instrumentality of a State acting in his or her official capacity." Section 511, added in 1990, is even more specific, stating that the Eleventh Amendment of the Constitution does not apply in copyright issues. Although these provisions seem quite clear, the courts have recently handed down decisions that directly contradict these sections. Indeed, one judge's decision went so far as to suggest that Congress had "overstepped its bounds" in writing these sections of the law (Lipinski, 2006). Obviously strong differences of opinion still exist regarding the effectiveness of the sovereign immunity defense.

POSSIBLE FUTURE DEVELOPMENTS

New bills have been introduced into the 110th and 111th Congresses which may impact libraries on some level if passed.

On February 27, 2007, Representative Rick Boucher (D-Virginia), along with Zoe Lofgren (D-California) and John Doolittle (R-California) introduced the "Freedom And Innovation Revitalizing U.S. Entrepreneurship Act of 2007" (FAIR USE Act) into the House of Representatives. This bill seeks to modify the Digital Millennium Copyright Act to allow removal of anti-circumvention devices for non-infringing uses such as skipping past commercial material on DVD's, using materials that are in the public domain, or other uses that are fair ones. The American Library Association and the American Association of Law Libraries have expressed their support for this bill (Foster, 2007).

The "Curb Illegal Downloading on College Campuses Act of 2007" was introduced in March of 2007, sponsored by Rep. Rick Keller (R-Florida) and Rep. Howard P. (Buck) McKeon of (R-California). (A similar bill had been previously introduced into the Senate in 2006 and been defeated.) Many college administrators feel that, should a bill like this be passed, federal student aid might be withheld for non-compliant colleges, because taking steps to combat piracy is one of the steps that would have to be taken in order for colleges to qualify for federal financial aid under the Higher Education Act (Read, 2007). Although not directly related to libraries, passage of such bill would place more of the responsibility for protecting the intellectual property interests of the private sector on the campus itself, a precedent which could be problematic for libraries down the road.

The “Intellectual Property Enhanced Criminal Enforcement Act” was introduced in the House of Representatives in July of 2007. This bill would impose stricter penalties for copyright infringements (Intellectual Property Enhanced Criminal Enforcement Act, 2007).

The “Intellectual Property Rights Enforcement Act” was introduced in the Senate in February of 2007, and in the House in September of 2007. The act speaks to problems with intellectual property on an international level, and addresses product counterfeiting and piracy. The act states that “Terrorist groups“ have “used the sale of counterfeit goods to finance their activities”. It also states that “funds generated from intellectual property theft have financed acts of terrorism”, and states that “The Department of the Treasury's Office of Terrorism and Financial Intelligence would be an effective tool in combating intellectual property theft,” which would expand the scope of copyright law enforcement (Intellectual Property Rights Enforcement Act, 2007).

The “Fair Copyright in Research Works Act” was introducted in Congress in February of 2009 in an attempt to undo the effects of Section 217 of the Omnibus Appropriations Act of 2009. Section 217 requires that researchers who are funded by the federal government make their research available to the public via the National Library of Medicine's PubMed Central within twelve months of publication (National Institute of Health, 2009). Publishers strongly support the Fair Copyright in Research Works Act because it would not only eliminate this free access, but would also prevent free public access to work funded by other federal agencies (Willinsky, 2009).

CONCLUSION

When librarians discuss copyright, one of the first sentiments often expressed is fear: fear of going against guidelines, of breaking the law, of litigation. Libraries are always ready to stand up for the right to read and freedom of speech, and to fight against intellectual surveillance and censorship. But when it comes to use of intellectual property by students, educators, and researchers -- use that is not only allowed, but encouraged, by section 8 of the U.S. Constitution -- librarians often stand by strict guidelines which were in part drawn up by the same special interests who clearly favor permission-seeking and payment by educational institutions as the primary model.

How real is the threat of litigation against a library? There are a number of compelling factors weighing in against the possibility of the publishing industry actually filing suits against educational or research institutions. First of all, there may be a reluctance on their part because historically Congress has viewed "respectable" stakeholders such as educational interests in a very positive light. United States code reflects this, as does case law (Olsen, 1989). This pattern is illustrated, for example, in the special provisions for libraries mentioned in the DMCA and the CTEA, in the creation of CONTU and CONFU, and also in case law (e.g., Williams & Witkin v. U.S. Government). Secondly, publishers historically make several attempts to engage in a dialogue with an educational institution regarding problem areas before filing an actual suit.

According to Siva Vaidhyanathan (*Copyrights and Copywrongs* and *The Anarchist in the Library)*, if an educator asks permission to use something, then it makes "this entire fair use calculus irrelevant. Why do we need section 107 at all if educators are just going to cower upon the advice of copyright experts on campus?" (Vaidhyanathan, 2007). "Copyright experts on campus" might be campus legal representation, or they may be the librarian everyone goes to when they have a copyright question. These representatives may fall back on the guidelines, using them as a maximum measure to ensure safety from litigation; or instead they may refer colleagues to the four points of fair use law and give them guidance in recent case law so that the colleagues can make their own educated decisions. There is a great deal of misinformation circulating about exactly what a library can and cannot do regarding fair use of materials (Waldman, et al, 2005).

Many legal experts have expressed similar feelings toward fair use and the idea of paying for permission to use materials for teaching, research, scholarship, or other fair uses. Wesley D. Blakeslee JD, Executive Director - Technology Transfer at Johns Hopkins University, has argued that even the "spontaneity" requirement of the CONTU guidelines on reserve materials is overused by libraries (O'Donnell and Parker, 2005). Fair use scholar Jonathan Franklin of the University of Washington believes that some institutions allow fear of legal action to drive their decisions regarding e-reserves (Carlson, 2005).

Copyright law is a murky and often-incomprehensible labyrinth of legalese, and yet safeguards have repeatedly been written into copyright law and court decisions to preserve the original spirit of the constitution regarding the use of copyrighted material. Libraries and educational institutions have historically been highly regarded by legislators and by the courts when addressing copyright issues, and organizations such as the American Library Association and Educause have been instrumental in maintaining our fair use rights. Libraries should be just as proactive, educating themselves in these issues and making their own educated decisions regarding the fair use of materials by the American public. L. Ray Patterson, professor of law and copyright scholar, who helped form the University of Georgia's copyright policy and who firmly believed in the fair use doctrine, said it best: "Librarians need to be as aggressive in protecting the right of fair use as the publishers are in seeking to destroy it" (Russell, 1999).

REFERENCES

Albanese, A. (2005). Battle brews over e-reserves. *Library Journal, 130* (9), 16-17.

Albanese, A. (2007). Down with e-reserves. *Library Journal, 132* (16), 36-38.

Albanese, A. (2008). Georgia State sued over e-reserves. *Library Journal,133* (9), 16-17.

Bono, M. (1998, October 7). Congressional Record House of Representatives, p.H9951. Retrieved October 10, 2007, from http://thomas.loc.gov

Bridges, A. (2007, May). E-reserves threatened at Cornell. *College and Research Libraries News, 68* (5), 317.

Carlson, S. (2005, April 22). Legal battle brews over availability of texts on online reserve at U. of California Library. *The Chronicle of Higher Education, 51* (33), A36.

Copyright Clearance Center (2007). International Licensing and Permissions. *Publishers.* Retrieved September 27, 2007, from http://www.copyright.com/ccc/viewPage.do?page Code=rh5

Copyright Clearance Center (2007). Copyright basics. *Copyright Central.* Retrieved September 23, 2007, from http://www.copyright.com/ccc/viewPage.do?pageCode=cr10-n

Cornell University Copyright Information Center (2007, September 12). Checklist for conducting a fair use analysis before using copyrighted materials. *Cornell Copyright Policies, Guidance, and Policy Interpretations.* Retrieved October 11, 2007, from http://www.copyright.cornell.edu/policy/Fair_Use_Checklist.pdf

Cornell University Law School (1991). Feist Publications, Inc. v. Rural Telephone Service Co., 499 U.S. 340. *Legal Information Institute.* Retrieved September 26, 2007, from http://www.law.cornell.edu/copyright/cases/499_US_340.htm

Cornell University Law School (1994). Campbell v. Acuff-Rose Music (92-1292), 510 U.S. 569. *Legal Information Institute.* Retrieved September 26, 2007, from http://www. law.cornell.edu/supct/search

Cornell University Law School (1994). Fogerty v. Fantasy, Inc. (92-1750), 510 U.S. 517. *Legal Information Institute.* Retrieved September 26, 2007, from http://www.law.cornell. edu/supct/search

Crews, K. (2002, September 30). New copyright law for distance education: the meaning and importance of the TEACH act. *ALA Washington Office.* Retrieved October 9, 2007, from http://www.ala.org/ala/washoff/woissues/ copyrightb/federallegislation/distanceed/teachsummary.pdf

Dames, K. M. (2005). Copyright Clearances: Fair Use Action and Apathy. *Online, 29* (5), 32-34. Retrieved September 18, 2007 the H. W. Wilson Library Literature database.

Folsom v. Marsh, 9 S. Ct. 342 (1841). Retrieved September 27, 2007, from http://www. faculty.piercelaw.edu/redfield/library/Pdf/case-folsom.marsh.pdf

Foster, A. (2007, March 9). Bill would ease limits on scholars' use of copyrighted works. *Chronicle of Higher Education, 53* (27), A38-A38.

Goldstein, P. (2003). *Copyright's highway.* Stanford, CA: Stanford University Press.

Gould, T., Lipinski, T., & Buchanan, E. (2005). Copyright policies and the deciphering of fair use in the creation of reserves at university libraries. *Journal of Academic Librarianship, 31*(3), 182-197.

Hafner, K. (2008). Publishers Sue Georgia State on Digital Reading Matter. (2008, April 16). *The New York Times*, p. C2(L).

Heller, J. S. (2004). *The librarian's copyright companion.* New York: William S. Hein & Co.

Hoffman, G.M. (2005). *Copyright in cyberspace 2.* New York: Neal Schuman.

Intellectual Property Enhanced Criminal Enforcement Act Of 2007, H.R.3155, 110th Cong. (2007). Retrieved October 22, 2007, from the Library of Congress Thomas database.

Intellectual Property Rights Enforcement Act of 2007, H.R.3578, 110th Cong. (2007). Retrieved October 22, 2007, from the Library of Congress - Thomas database.

Kosinski, A. & Newman, C. (1999). What's So Fair About Fair Use? *Journal of the Copyright Society of the USA, 46* (4), 513-530.

Kranich, N. (1984). *Copyright policies in ACRL libraries.* Washington, DC: Association of Research Libraries.

Lipinski, T. (2006). *Complete Copyright Liability Handbook for Librarians and Educators.* New York: Neal Schuman.

National Institute of Health (2009). *The Omnibus Appropriations Act of 2009 makes the NIH public access policy permanent.* Retrieved April 23, 2009, from http://grants.nih.gov/ grants/guide/notice-files/NOT-OD-09-071.html

O'Donnell, M. & Parker, C. W. (2005, May 27). How colleges can navigate the thicket of federal regulations. *The Chronicle of Higher Education, 51* (38), B5.

Olsen, T. P. (1989). The iron law of consensus. *Journal of the Copyright Society of the USA, 36* (2), 109-137.

Patterson, L. R., & Lindberg, S.W. (1991). *The nature of copyright.* Athens, GA: University of Georgia Press.

Pike, G. H. (2006, December). Abolishing fair use? *Information Today, 23* (11), 21-23. Retrieved September 13, 2007 from the Ebsco Academic Search Premier database.

Pike, G. H. (2007, July-August). A stronger fair use doctrine? *Information Today, 24* (7), 15-16.

Public Law No. 105-298, 105th Cong. Rec. I298.105 (1998) (enacted). Retrieved October 5, 2007 from http://thomas.loc.gov/cgi-bin/query/z?c105:s.505.enr:

Public Law No. 105-304, 105th Cong. Rec. H10048-10073 (1998) (enacted). Retrieved September 22, 2007, from http://www.access.gpo.gov/index.html

Read, B. (2007, October 19). Congress again tries to force colleges to curb student music and video piracy. *Chronicle of Higher Education*, *54* (8), A30.

Russell, C. (1999, December). Users' rights in copyright: an interview with Ray Patterson. *ALA Washington Office - Copyright Articles & Interviews.* Retrieved September 20, 2007, from http://www.ala.org/ala/washoff/ woissues/copyrightb/copyrightarticle

United States Copyright Office (2003). United States Code – Title 17. Retrieved September 27, 2007, from http://www.copyright.gov/title17/

United States Copyright Office (1995). Circular 21 – Reproduction of copyrighted works by educators and librarians. Retrieved September 22, 2007, from http://www.copyright.gov/ circs/circ21.pdf

United States House of Representatives (2004, September 20). United States Constitution. Retrieved September 24, 2007, from http://www.house.gov/house/Constitution/ Constitution.html

Vaidhyanathan, S. (2007, July 7). Fair use in (in)action. *SIVACRACY.NET: Siva Vaidhyanathan's Weblog*. Retrieved September 4, 2007, from http://www.nyu.edu/ classes/siva/2004/07/fair-use-inaction.html

Waldman, M, Goldberg, D., & Heins, M. (2005). *Will fair use survive?* New York: Brennan Center for Justice - NYU School of Law. Retrieved September

15, 2007 from http://www.fepproject.org/policyreports/WillFairUseSurvive.pdf

Wilinsky, J. (2009). The publishers' pushback against NIH's public access and scholarly publishing sustainability. *PLOS Biology Journal.* Retrieved April 21, 2009 from http://www.pubmedcentral.nih.gov/articlerender.fcgi?artid=2631074

In: Academic Librarianship in the 21st Century ISBN: 978-1-60456-865-3
Editors: C. M.Garcia and T. A.Flores

Chapter 5

INCREASING INFORMATION RETRIEVAL THROUGH SUBJECT ACCESS IMPROVEMENTS

Susan E. Russell and Jie Huang
University of Oklahoma Libraries, Norman, Oklahoma, USA

ABSTRACT

Library of Congress subject headings (LCSH) have been a very important component of bibliographic records for many years. The use of tightly controlled vocabulary to create specific subject headings provides greater precision in subject searches to help direct patrons to the most relevant materials. Yet subject searches are still the most difficult and problematic search for many patrons who do not understand LCSH structure and have difficulty identifying the exact keywords necessary to complete a comprehensive search.

Cataloging librarians evaluate and identify areas where bibliographic records can be enhanced to provide patrons with as many access points as possible. Ideally, the cataloger evaluates items and then assigns specific subject headings and broader, less-specific subject headings that can be narrowed in scope through the addition of subdivisions. This process increases accessibility to materials by offering more ways to locate them. These subject searches will not provide patrons with a comprehensive list of every item available to them unless these broader subject headings are assigned consistently to materials. Ensuring consistency in subject headings can be difficult because many items are processed through vendor records, shared cataloging databases and localized copy-cataloging practices. While these methods speed up the processing of materials, they do not provide a step where additional subject access points can be consistently added.

A study of subject searches entered by patrons at the University of Oklahoma Libraries over the course of two semesters should allow identification of problematic areas and provide insight into search patterns among the types of subject headings used most. This analysis should also illustrate discrepancies between the keywords used by patrons and the corresponding LCSH for failed subject searches.

We hope to provide feasible suggestions for future improvements in assignment and usage of LCSH to make them easier to use, understand, and apply. Eventual goals of this study include: (1) incorporating less-controlled vocabulary that is more user-friendly through broader usage of cross-references; (2) updating and adding new LCSH more quickly to reflect advancements in technology, evolving research and study disciplines, and current events and nomenclature; and (3) developing consistency checks to allow enhancement of bibliographic records to provide more accessibility to materials through subject searches.

INTRODUCTION

Libraries contain a variety of materials on an abundance of subjects. The library exists for patrons to find information and the primary purpose of its catalog is to create an index of all the library's holdings and collections so patrons can know what is available to them and how it can be accessed. A library's Online Public Access Catalog (OPAC) is its introduction to patrons; the ability to search easily and effectively is essential to user satisfaction. In many cases, a new user's level of searching satisfaction will determine whether or not he/she will become repeat users or seek out other avenues to meet their information needs, even from less reliable sources. For academic libraries, this is particularly disturbing since their primary mission is to support the studies, teaching and research of their students and faculty through the acquisition and dissemination of scholarly materials.

With the advent of the Web search engine, the patrons' search behavior has changed greatly. OPAC expectations have also dramatically shifted (Yu & Young, 2004; Carstens & Buchanan, 2004). Some research has revealed that patrons prefer to use an Internet search engine, such as Google, over seeking help from librarians if they cannot get the results from the library's online catalog quickly (Antell & Huang, 2008). Other patrons only search for information they need on the Web without ever consulting the library's online catalog or other resources (Carstens & Buchanan, 2004; Gardner & Eng, 2005). To many patrons, especially undergraduate students, Internet searching seems much more convenient than searching a library OPAC. They can type in any general word or phrase and in most cases an abundance of full-text information is quickly available to them.

From this, the debate among librarians has escalated that something must be changed if libraries are to continue their role as a primary source for information, and three groups of thought have emerged. The first group strongly contends that the Library of Congress subject headings (LCSH) system remains viable for the specificity it brings to subject searches based on strictly controlled-subject vocabularies with precise cross-referencing and tight authority control and that this rigid continuity provides a standardized foundation for shared cataloging as well as compatibility between OPACs and other library databases (Mann, 2003; Beall, 2006). For them, bibliographic instruction is still the key to better understanding of how the system works and what the user must do to search more effectively. However, for many years now, study after study confirms that the current OPAC system is not being utilized to its full potential; fewer than fifty percent of patrons are performing subject searches with the correct terminology (Drabenstott, et al., 1999).

The second group believes that technological developments mean subject searches could and should be modified to make them more useful to patrons who are less familiar with the LCSH system and that a less tightly controlled system would be more functional in today's environment. It would allow successful subject searches with minimal participation or forethought from the patrons (Dean, 2004; Fischer, 2005). For them, the OPAC should be completely redesigned into a Web search engine that looks and functions like Google to encourage patrons. However, Web search engines, such as Google, are not without disappointment. Carstens & Buchanan (2004) listed inaccurate or biased information, a commercial nature, large and unmanageable retrieval sets, and the small amount of scholarly information that is actually available for free as some of the well-known limitations of Web search engines. They also pointed out that although Web search engines are the best tools for finding certain types of information, the academic library remains the best place to find scholarly information and librarians must now focus on developing an academic search engine which continues to provide precise, accurate, quality searches with the ease of use, quick access, and convenience of a Web search engine. This description of a modified OPAC which combines the best of both models encompasses the third group of thought (Fugmann, 2000; Nowick & Mering, 2003; Anderson & Hofmann, 2006).

Guidance through bibliographic instruction is still needed and should be improved in the academic library to direct students, particularly undergraduates, on how to go deeper into OPAC searching capabilities (Antell & Huang, 2008). This guidance needs to be brief, self-explanatory, and more discipline-specific allowing users to explore both onsite and from a distance so they will stay with their OPAC search and not miss out on what is actually available to them through the library. But the OPAC and the rules of cataloging that govern it must also continue to grow and evolve more quickly along with technology to insure that it is providing optimum support to its patrons and adequately reflecting the richness of the collection it represents (Fidel, 2000; Olson & Boll, 2001; Trendler, 2001).

Professional catalogers evaluate and identify areas where bibliographic records can be enhanced to provide patrons with as many access points as possible. Many of the past technological and manpower limitations are no longer a problem. OPACs now have more programming options combined with adequate space for more comprehensive coverage that was not possible with the card catalog or even the beginning OPAC systems. In addition, many of the cataloger's routine duties have been reduced or eliminated through technology, localized copy-cataloging practices, shared cataloging databases, and outsourced shelf-ready materials with vendor-supplied records. The cataloger now has more time to go back and enhance existing bibliographic records to make them more accessible—enough projects to last a lifetime—but must also insure that newly processed items are being added to the OPAC with adequate and consistent access points (Lam, 2000; Marshall, 2003; Ashman, 2006). This process will dramatically increase accessibility to library materials by offering more ways to locate them. LCSH have been a very important component of bibliographic records for many years. The use of tightly controlled vocabulary and cross-references to create specific subject headings provides greater precision in subject searches to help direct patrons to the most relevant materials (Carstens & Buchanan, 2004). Yet subject searches are still the most difficult and problematic search for many patrons who do not understand LCSH structure and have difficulty identifying the exact keywords necessary to complete a comprehensive search (Drabenstott, 1999; Olson & Boll, 2001). Inverted headings such as "Roads, Roman" and "Drawing, Psychology of" can be elusive to the patron necessitating thorough use of cross-references. While LCSH authority control provides a cross-reference for "Roman roads" leading to the correct terminology in the first example, it does not provide "Psychology of drawing" as a cross-reference for the second example, which seems like a practical search term. There are no cross-references or scope notes given in the LCSH authority control for "Contemporary, The, in literature" or "Contemporary, The, in art" which would seem likely candidates for further assistance.

Lam (2000) pointed out that the limited number of subject headings assigned to monographs as well as the practice of providing a more general subject heading for a monograph that covers several more specific topics also results in very inadequate subject access to monographs. This is particularly true for multi-volume sets. For example, *Corpus of early keyboard music* is a large, multi-volume set. Held by 62 institutions including ours, the WorldCat record is very brief with "Harpsichord music" as the single general subject heading. Local enhancement of this record in our OPAC has greatly expanded potential access points through five additional MARC tag 650 subject headings that more fully represent the variety of material included in the set.

Another common criticism is that Library of Congress should be updating and adding new subject headings more quickly to reflect advancements in technology, evolving research and study disciplines, and current events and nomenclature. Yet a comparative study of superseded LCSH in online catalogs by Ashman (2006) revealed that in many cases older headings had not been completely replaced and were still present in varying degrees. This data indicates that the problem of outdated subject headings usage often exists at the local level even after it has been addressed in the LCSH creating a lack of standardization in subject search access points.

Every discipline has terminology that is specific to its subject, and it is the library cataloger's job to assign LCSH which will provide the greatest access to these materials. In some cases this can be rather difficult as the LCSH which best matches the item can be rather different from the everyday language used to describe it. For instance, the LCSH "High interest-low vocabulary books" then provides several cross-references such as "Easy readers", "Easy reading books, and "Easy-to-read books" to help lead the patron from the commonly used name to the correct search term. However, in the case of "Paratransit services" it is less obvious since the two cross-references "Demand responsive transportation" and "Dial-a-ride" are very specific, less commonly used terminology. In a comparison study between LCSH and key terms from the National Council of Teachers of Mathematics (NCTM) mathematics standards, Plummer (2006) concluded that controlled vocabulary was more helpful than keyword searching in theory but was sometimes hindered by outdated terminology.

Ethnology and ethnic groups present a strong argument for the value of controlled vocabulary over keyword searching. Beall (2006) found keyword searching did not provide the optimal search results that databases which utilized controlled vocabulary such as LCSH produced because most individual ethnic groups are known by many different names. OPACs which utilize LCSH are still the most efficient system for organizing and quickly finding information about ethnology and ethnic groups. The authority heading selected as the main heading is generally the one that is most commonly used in reference sources with several cross references for the variant forms.

Many librarians are aware of the problematic subject searches that patrons frequently encounter and continue to do research on this topic. One of the most commonly used research tools is transaction log analysis because it provides specific information about how the OPAC is being used to search and retrieve information. Librarians have been using transaction logs to study user search patterns with online catalogs since the late 1960s (Peters, 1993; Sandore, 1993; Blecic et al., 1998; Graham, 2004; Villen-Rueda et al., 2007). Through systematic examination of each search command by a patron and the results retrieved, it is possible to obtain data about how well the patron understands and is able to use the OPAC in locating the information needed. There are many uses for data collected through transaction logs. From the data, librarians can identify areas and concepts that need to be emphasized in online tutorials and bibliographic instruction classes. Reviewing OPAC transaction logs can also provide invaluable information to cataloging librarians about the searching habits and patterns of their OPAC users and how they can improve accessibility through bibliographic record enhancement.

Utilizing transaction log analysis, a study of subject searches entered by patrons at the University of Oklahoma Libraries over the course of two semesters was carried out to help identify problematic areas and provide some insight into search patterns among the types of subject headings used most. This analysis would illustrate discrepancies between the keywords used by patrons and the corresponding LCSH for failed subject searches in our OPAC system. From this we hope to provide feasible suggestions for future improvements in assignment and usage of LCSH to make them easier to use, understand, and apply.

METHODOLOGY

The methodology used for this research consists of two parts. The first part is, to some extent, similar to the one used for another research project, conducted by Antell & Huang (2008) at the University of Oklahoma Libraries, on how reference librarians can help patrons use subject searches in an effective way to access the information they need. For the present research project, we analyze transaction logs in order to find out how catalogers can improve the results of subject searches. The data used for this research were retrieved from the transaction logs during the academic year 2006-2007 from the University of

Oklahoma Libraries' online catalog system. Since the transaction logs included the searches conducted by the library personnel during its work time, we tried to retrieve the data randomly from different time periods during a day and different days during a week to cover the searches conducted by different groups of users. The three time periods, which almost cover the library's opening hours, were used to divide a day: 8:00 am-2:00 pm; 2:00 pm-8:00 pm; 8:00 pm-2:00 am. The days chosen for data retrieval included weekdays and weekends. Through the retrieval of 31 sample periods during the year, we collected 134,801 transaction logs. After eliminating the "login" transactions that do not count as actual information searches, the total number of transaction logs of real searches was 73,784. Among these searches, many used the Online Computer Library Center (OCLC) record numbers, and they were therefore most likely conducted by the library staff. This is because the transaction logs obtained during daytime on the workdays included many searches conducted by the library personnel, such as the staff in the Cataloging Department. Those searches often use the OCLC record numbers to access the records for cataloging or acquisition purposes. To better understand the patrons' search behavior, 36,004 transaction logs of this type were also removed from the total usable data. After these first two steps, the total number of transaction logs used for this research analysis became 37,780. Although we fully understand that other types of transaction logs also contain some searches done by the library staff, it is impossible at this point to separate them from the searches done by the patrons. Since most data were collected from the periods other than the work time, the remaining types of data should be accurate enough for this research.

All the useable data were analyzed by type of search (keyword, title, subject, etc.) first to determine which type of search patrons used the most and how often they would use the subject search. Then the transaction logs of subject search were analyzed to see how many correct LCSH were used in the searches. All 1,759 subject terms retrieved were checked by comparing with the LCSH authority records. Analyses were also performed to determine how the results were retrieved. Our first question is: With the searches that resulted in any number of hits other than zero, did they result from using correct LCSH or from matching keywords in the subjects? All searches with zero hit were analyzed to find out the reason why patrons had not found what they needed. Our next question then is: Were they caused by typographical errors, wrong subject terms, or lack of the materials they needed?

We also labeled the searches as either "successful" or "unsuccessful" according to if they had resulted in any number of hits at all for the purposes of those researches: those that had resulted in any number of hits were considered as "successful" whereas those that had resulted in no hits at all were regarded as "unsuccessful". Nevertheless, we completely understand the limitation of this method. That is, among the searches with results, some had large numbers of hits. From the transaction logs alone, it was difficult to find out if the patrons were satisfied with those large numbers of results and would consider them as successful searches or not. In effect, satisfaction can only be decided by the patrons after they look at the results and, for that reason, it can only be found out through communication with the patrons. It cannot be decided based simply on the number of results. With only transaction logs available to us at this point, we feel this is the best we can do for this type of research.

The second part of the methodology is simulation of the searches conducted on the Internet search engines, such as Google, by patrons. Many articles have talked about the phenomenon that patrons, especially undergraduate and graduate students, like to turn to Internet search engines to find materials if they don't find them in the library's online catalogs. Are the Internet search engines more helpful than library's online catalogs? Should the LCSH or other controlled vocabulary be replaced by uncontrolled vocabulary? Will subject with uncontrolled vocabulary make subject searches easier? To compare ease, effectiveness and accuracy of information retrieval between the Internet search engines and our library online catalog, twenty search terms from the transaction logs were randomly selected and used to conduct simulated searches on Google.

RESULTS

As mentioned in the methodology section above, 37,780 searches were analyzed. They were divided into five categories, as shown in Figure 1 below: Keyword search, title search, author search, subject search, and other search. Besides monograph titles, "title search" also includes periodical titles and series titles. "Other search" consists of searches using International Standard Book Number (ISBN) and International Standard Serial Number (ISSN). The result shows that the keyword search is the most popular method used by many patrons. It had 17,626 transaction logs and made up 47% of the total searches. It is then followed respectively by 8,973 title searches, 4,714 other searches, 4,708 author searches, and 1,759 subject searches (see Figure 1). Subject search was only close to 5% of the total searches. It was the method used the least by patrons.

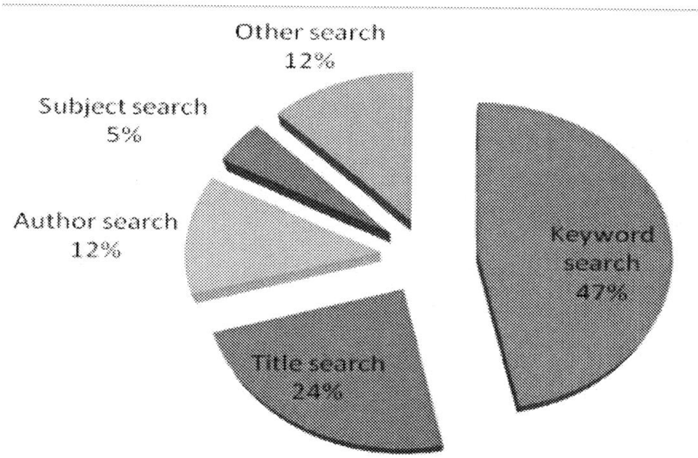

Figure 1. The percentages of various search types

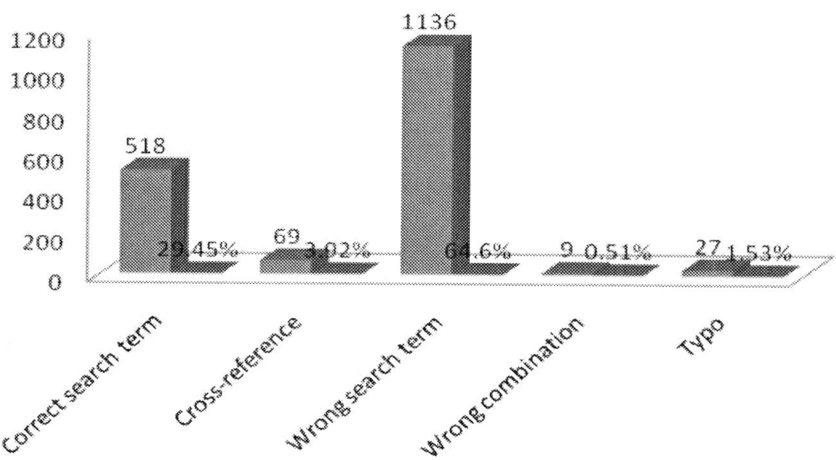

Figure 2. The numbers and percentages of various types of subject searches

Of the total of 1,759 subject searches, only 587 used the correct LCSH, including 69 cross-reference searches. It only reached 33.37% of the total subject searches. Other subject searches involved wrong subject terms (1,136 transactions, 64.6%), wrong combinations (9 transactions, 0.51%), or typographical errors (27 transactions, 1.53%) (see Figure 2). Since both wrong combinations and typographical errors only made up very small percentages, they can be ignored for our purposes. Through comparing the two main categories, correct search term and wrong search term, the result showed that the transactions with wrong subject terms almost doubled the searches with correct subject terms.

Then the total subject searches were analyzed by the number of hits received. The results showed that 883 out of the total 1,759 searches, that is 50.2% of the total searches, received at least one hit; 876 that is 49.8% of the total searches, resulted in zero hit (see Figure 3).

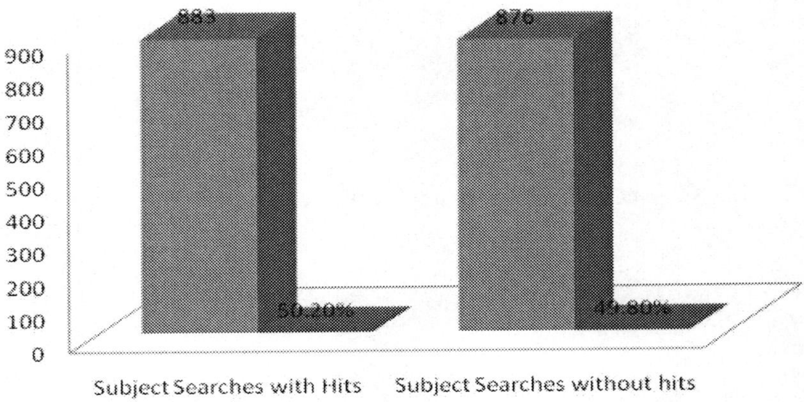

Figure 3. The numbers and percentages of the subject searches with and without hits

To find out how the hits were retrieved, we performed analyses to see how many correct subject terms that completely matched LCSH were actually used in these searches. After looking at each search, we found that only 428 subject terms used were correct, which is around 48.47%. The rest of the searches (455 searches, 51.53%) used wrong search terms (see Figure 4). They resulted in hits merely because their search terms match some keywords in the LCSH assigned to the records. Among the 876 searches with zero hit, only 31 searches, or 3.54%, used correct subject terms. These searches did not retrieve any results because the library collections do not have the materials that exactly match the requests, or because the cross-references are not properly linked to the bibliographic records. The other reasons for not being able to get any hits are wrong combinations of subject terms and typographical errors (see Figure 5). Obviously, the results shown above were not good. They revealed that subject search is still the most problematic to most patrons.

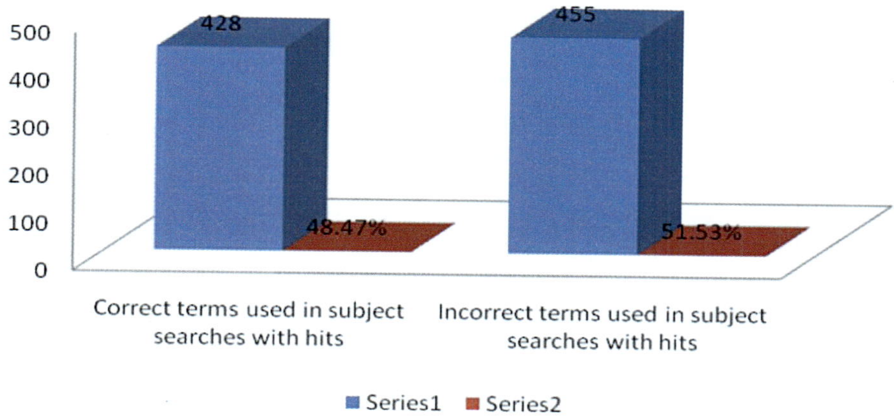

Figure 4. The numbers and percentages of the correct and incorrect terms used in subject searches with hits

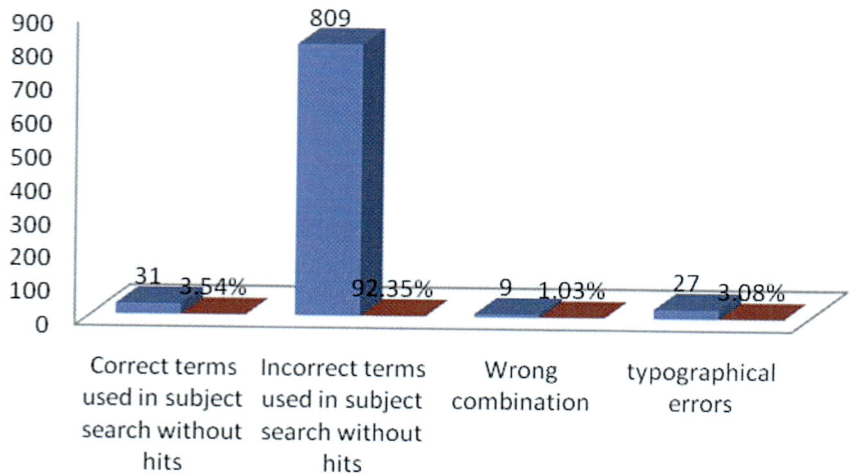

Figure 5. The numbers and percentages of the types of searches without hits

The searches conducted on Google always retrieved large number of hits, usually over 100,000. Some search terms with common words even yielded over one million hits. The information received from the Internet search engine was unmanageable. To reduce the number of hits, the search terms were then put into quotation marks so that the whole phrase would be matched instead of each separate word. With this search method, the hits retrieved were reduced dramatically. For example, the first term used in the Google search was "naturally fractured gas condensate reservoirs". It retrieved over 122,000 hits. After the term was put in quotation marks, the hits decreased to 34. But if the search terms consisted of common words, such as "health career", the number of hits was still over 100,000 even after quotation marks were used to make the search engine find information which matched the whole phrase instead of individual words. The comparison of the results retrieved from Google and from the OU online catalog clearly revealed that patrons can always find information through the Internet search engines, but they have to spend lots of time sorting it. Much of it was websites, proposals, titles, or course agendas, etc., which only presents a very small percentage of scholarly work. When patrons used subject search terms which did not match LCSH, the searches conducted on the OU libraries' online catalog still retrieved some hits if the patrons chose subject search with keyword. It is simply because the system presented all records that had the keywords within their subject headings. If patrons chose the exact subject search, then those search terms that didn't match the LCSH resulted in zero hits. Although the hits retrieved from the online catalog were much lower than from Google, the effectiveness and precision were much higher.

CONCLUSION

Initially, Internet searching seems much more convenient than searching a library OPAC. But many times when you begin looking through this material, it is disappointing to find that as you click on each one they are often the same text verbatim with the only distinguishing feature being the background, font, layout, etc. The text has been taken from one primary source, and then this information has been duplicated online over and over by additional sites that become superfluous sources for the exact same material. The same pattern can also be found when searching for maps, diagrams, photos, etc. The searcher must open and look at each of these sites to determine which ones are verbatim information and which provide additional information. So even though fewer hits may be retrieved for the same search in an OPAC, each of these hits will be different items of information since multiple copies of the same item are attached to one bibliographic record. From this it would seem that free text Internet searching is great for a quick answer but not always helpful for deeper research or study of a given topic unless employing more sophisticated searching techniques as in the OPAC (Fugmann, 2000).

The ability to subject search easily and effectively in an OPAC is essential to user satisfaction, and research indicates that patrons' search behavior has changed significantly over the past few years. OPAC expectations have also risen with the advent of the Web search engine, and librarians are now faced with the task of developing an academic search engine which continues to provide precise, accurate, quality searches with the ease of use, quick access, and convenience of a Web search engine. Cataloging librarians must reevaluate their role in helping to improve the results of subject searches in this new environment by providing feasible suggestions for future improvements in assignment and usage of LCSH to make them easier to use, understand, and apply.

To provide more accessibility to materials through subject searches, consistency checks must be incorporated at the local level to insure enhancement of existing bibliographic records takes place as needed while insuring that newly processed items are being added to the OPAC with adequate and consistent access points. Three areas that should be improved at the local level are: (1) addition of cross-references for commonly used names and terms to discipline-specific subject headings that are frequently used within the university's curriculum; (2) addition of direct order cross-references for items with inverted subject headings that are identified as problematic for patrons; and (3) updating and adding new LCSH quickly and consistently.

More utilization of 6XX fields is needed to provide avenues for incorporating less-controlled vocabulary that is more user-friendly through broader usage of cross-references and keywords. It would be helpful to have thesauri-controlled vocabulary for various disciplines that cross-reference students to the correct subject search terms. MARC tag 654 for "Subject Added Entry—Faceted Topical Terms" could be used to allow topical subject terms to be constructed from a faceted vocabulary such as the *Art and Architecture Thesaurus*. Gil-Leiva & Alonson-Arroyo (2007) suggested that keywords supplied by authors of scientific articles could be used to enhance keyword within subject heading searches for patrons. MARC tag 653 for "Index Term—Uncontrolled—Indexes terms not derived from a controlled thesaurus or subject heading system like LCSH" could also be used to add keywords which reflect advancements in technology, evolving research and study disciplines, and current events and nomenclature to existing bibliographic records for specific subject terms that are not found in LCSH.

Fidel (2000) suggests that academic libraries could improve course-related subject searches by adding relevant vocabulary lists to the online catalog. By typing in the title of the course for which he or she needs information, the student would then be provided with a list of applicable search terms. MARC tag 690 for "Local Subject Heading" could be used to input course titles for large undergraduate courses offered each semester (e.g. Introduction to World Music) which would direct students to materials essential to the course.

This study provides some feasible suggestions for future improvements in assignment and usage of LCSH to make them easier to use, understand, and apply. Follow-up research should be carried out in the future and we hope to start a pilot program that would implement some of these suggestions in a selected discipline. After one year's experiment, we can collect data from transaction logs and analyze the results using the same method to see if any improvement has occurred.

Subject search is an important tool for patrons to find the information they need in a library's OPAC. Cataloging librarians should continue working with reference librarians to make searches easier and more effective for patrons.

REFERENCES

Anderson, J. D., & Hofmann, M. A. (2006). A Fully Faceted Syntax for Library of Congress Subject Headings. *Cataloging & Classification Quarterly*, 43, 7-38.

Antell, K., & Huang, J. (2008). Subject Searching Success: Transaction Logs, Patron Perceptions, and Implications for Library Instruction. *Reference & User Services Quarterly*, 48, 68-76.

Ashman, A. B. (2006). The Persistence of Superseded Subject Headings in Online Catalogs. *Technical Services Quarterly*, 24, 27-34.

Beall, J. (2006). Ethnic Groups and Library of Congress Subject Headings. *Colorado Libraries*, 32, 37-44.

Blecic, D. D., Bangalore, N. S., Dorsch, J. L., Henderson, C. L., Koenig, M. H., & Weller, A. C. (1998). Using Transaction Log Analysis to Improve OPAC Retrieval Results. *College & Research Libraries*, 59, 39-50.

Carstens, T., & Buchanan, H. (2004). The Future of the Catalog: A User-Friendly Academic Search Engine. *Technical Services Quarterly*, 22, 37-47.

Dean, R. J. (2004). FAST: Development of Simplified Headings for Metadata. *Cataloging & Classification Quarterly*, 39, 331-352.

Drabenstott, K. M., Simcox, S., & Fenton, E. G. (1999). End-User Understanding of Subject Headings in Library Catalogs. *Library Resources & Technical Services*, 43, 140-160.

Fidel, R. (2000). The User-Centered Approach: How We Got Here. In W. J. Wheeler (Ed.), *Saving the User's Time through Subject Access Innovation* (pp. 79-99). Champaign: Publications Office, Graduate School of Library and Information Science.

Fischer, K. S. (2005). Critical Views of LCSH, 1990-2001: The Third Bibliographic Essay. *Cataloging & Classification Quarterly*, 41, 63-109.

Fugmann, R. (2000). Obstacles to Progress in Mechanized Subject Access and the Necessity of a Paradigm Change. In W. J. Wheeler (Ed.), *Saving the User's Time through Subject Access Innovation* (pp. 7-45). Champaign: Publications Office, Graduate School of Library and Information Science.

Gardner, S. & Eng, S. (2005). What Students Want: Generation Y and the Changing Function of the Academic Library. *Portal: Libraries and the Academy*, 5, 405-420.

Gil-Leiva, I. & Alonson-Arroyo, A. (2007). Keywords Given by Authors of Scientific Articles in Database Descriptors. *Journal of the American Society for Information Science and Technology*, 58, 1175-1187.

Graham, R. Y. (2004). Subject No-hits Searches in an Academic Library Online Catalog: An Exploration of Two Potential Ameliorations. *College Research Libraries*, 65, 36-54.

Lam, V. (2000). Enhancing Subject Access to Monographs in Online Public Access Catalogs: Table of Contents Added to Bibliographic Records. In W. J. Wheeler (Ed.), *Saving the User's Time through Subject Access Innovation* (pp. 162-172). Champaign: Publications Office, Graduate School of Library and Information Science.

Mann, T. (2003). Why LC Subject Headings are More Important Than Ever. *American Libraries*, 34, 52-54.

Marshall, L. (2003). Specific and Generic Subject Headings: Increasing Subject Access to Library Materials. *Cataloging & Classification Quarterly*, 36, 59-87.

Nowick, E. A., & Mering, M. (2003). Comparisons Between Internet Users' Free-text Queries and Controlled Vocabularies: A Case Study in Water Quality. *Technical Services Quarterly*, 21, 15-32.

Olson, H. A., & Boll, J. J. (2001). *Subject Analysis in Online Catalogs* (2nd ed). Englewood, CO: Libraries Unlimited.

Peters, T. A. (1993). The History and Development of Transaction Log Analysis. *Library Hi Tech*, 11, 41-66.

Plummer, K. A. (2006). Mathematics Subject Headings for the PreK-12 Community: A Comparison of Key Terms from the National Council of Teachers of Mathematics (NCTM) Mathematics Standards to ERIC Thesaurus Descriptors and the Library of Congress Subject Headings. *Cataloging & Classification Quarterly*, 42, 59-73.

Sandore, B. (1993). Applying the Results of Transaction Log Analysis. *Library Hi Tech*, 42, 87-97.

Trendler, A. E. (2001). The Rules Have Changed: Library of Congress Subject Headings for Art and Architecture *Art Documentation*, 20, 24-29.

Villen-Rueda, L., Senso, J. A., & Moya-Anegon, F. (2007). The Use of OPAC in a Large Academic Library: A Transactional Log Analysis Study of Subject Searching. *Journal of Academic Librarianship*, 33, 327-337.

Yu, H., & Young, M. (2004). The Impact of Web Search Engines on Subject Searching in OPAC. *Information Technology and Libraries* 23, 168-180.

In: Academic Librarianship in the 21st Century
Editors: C. M.Garcia and T. A.Flores
ISBN: 978-1-60456-865-3

Chapter 6

AN OVERVIEW OF LIS OPEN ACCESS LITERATURE

Ángel Borrego*, Candela Ollé and Marta Somoza
University of Barcelona, Faculty of Library and Information Science
Melcior de Palau, 140, 08014 Barcelona, Spain

ABSTRACT

An overview of the open access literature in Library and Information Science (LIS) is offered. A list of 78 scholarly journals in LIS that are freely available electronically was compiled through the Directory of Open Access Journals (DOAJ). Characteristics of the journals—language, publisher, start year and frequency—were analysed. For each journal its coverage by three major abstracting and indexing services in the field— Library and Information Science Abstracts (LISA), Library, Information Science & Technology Abstracts (LISTA) and Library Literature and Information Science Full Text (LibLit)—was determined. Additionally a list of 48 open access digital repositories in LIS was obtained from the Directory of Open Access Repositories (OpenDOAR). Features of the repositories—language, software, size and contents—were analysed.

* Corresponding author: borrego@ub.edu

INTRODUCTION

During the last few years there has been a dramatic increase in the number of scholarly electronic journals freely available through the Internet. Although in many cases they are just the electronic version of a journal previously available in paper, the facilities of digital edition have motivated the birth of numerous new journals. In many cases the editors of these new journals have opted for offering their contents in open access without charging its readers.

This phenomenon has raised concerns about the quality of the contents of some of these new journals. The low cost of a digital edition has allowed the publication of journals that have an ephemeral life as a consequence of not reaching a minimum level of quality.

This chapter presents an overview of open access literature in Library and Information Science (LIS). The characteristics of 78 journals listed in the Directory of Open Access Journals (DOAJ, http://www.doaj.org) were analysed and its presence in three major abstracting and indexing services was determined. Additionally, the features of 48 open access digital repositories listed in the Directory of Open Access Repositories (OpenDOAR, http://www.opendoar.org) were analysed.

Until now most of the studies about the impact of open access journals have adopted a bibliometric focus, analysing citations obtained by journals and articles published in open access. The main hypothesis is that as these journals and articles are offered without any charge they are more visible than subscribed content and receive a greater degree of attention and citations. Craig et al. (2007) have recently published a critical review on the matter.

Leaving aside citation studies, Fosmire and Young (2000) analysed the presence of 213 free scholarly electronic journals in the catalogues of holding institutions on OCLC and in some major abstracting and indexing databases. The authors found that despite approximately half of the titles being indexed by major vendors, access levels in catalogues were fairly low and decreased dramatically with size of the institution.

Jacsó (2001) also studied the coverage of ten LIS electronic journals by six online databases. According to him (p. 47), "I am certainly not alone believing that many of the electronic journals in library and information science have far more relevant and timely articles for today's librarians and information specialists than many of the traditional scholarly LIS journals."

Finally, Hawkings (2001) performed a bibliometric analysis of 28 electronic journals in LIS. He concluded that most of the articles in these journals originated from the United States and were authored by a single person. The publication rate was at that time around 250 articles per year and it was increasing. Six online databases covered these electronic journals but Social Sciences Citation Index did not cover any of them at that time.

Sources for the Identification of Open Access Journals and Repositories

A list of 78 scholarly journals in the field of LIS that are freely available electronically was compiled through the Directory of Open Access Journals (DOAJ) in September 2007. Three of these journals had been discontinued and replaced by new journals that were also included in the Directory. The final set of journals was therefore reduced to 75.

For each journal, the DOAJ provides its title, URL, ISSN and EISSN, if applicable, subject, publisher, language, keywords and start year. Twenty-five of the journals are "DOAJ Content" which means that tables of contents are available and individual articles are searchable through a search engine. A link to the full text is also offered.

This list of open access journals in LIS is exhaustive. Searching for journals in LIS in Ulrich's Periodicals Directory offers a list of 3,759 journals, 63 of them (1.7%) categorized as open access.

The degree of agreement between DOAJ and Ulrich's Periodicals Directory is very high confirming thus the exactitude of the data. Only four of the journals categorized in Ulrich's Periodicals Directory as "open access" were not included in DOAJ. In one of the cases the journal had ceased. The others might have not satisfied the selection criteria established by DOAJ. Even more surprising is the fact that sixteen of the journals indexed in DOAJ were not included in Ulrich's Periodicals Directory, especially taking into account that these journals are not necessarily the newest ones and only four of them had been created in the last three years (2005-2007).

According to Ulrich's Periodicals Directory, 37 out of these 59 journals (62.7%) are peer reviewed.

Additionally, a set of 48 open access digital repositories with LIS content was compiled through the Directory of Open Access Repositories (OpenDOAR, http://www.opendoar.org). For each repository, OpenDOAR provides the organization responsible for the repository, a short description, OAI-PMH, software, size, subjects, content, languages and policies.

CHARACTERISTICS OF OPEN ACCESS JOURNALS IN LIS

Language

Fifty-six of the 75 journals included in DOAJ (74.7%) are monolingual while 19 (25.3%) publish contents in some two to five languages. Obviously, in most of the cases the distribution of contents into the different languages is not balanced.

As shown in Figure 1 the great majority of journals (59 journals, 78.7%) publish articles in English. Additionally, 14 journals (18.7%) publish contents in Spanish and 10 journals (13.3%) include articles in Portuguese. The total number of journals computed in the figure exceeds 75 as several journals are multilingual.

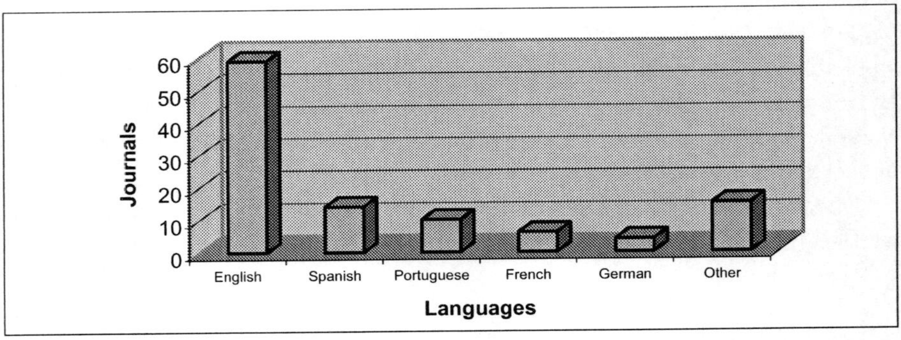

Figure 1. Number of LIS open access journals by language.

If we compare the distribution of LIS open access journals by language with the global distribution of LIS journals by language we observe a severe disagreement in the case of Spanish and Portuguese. As shown in Table 1, although, according to Ulrich's Periodicals Directory, only 5.5% of LIS journals are in Spanish, 18.7% of LIS open access journals are in this language. In the same way, although only 1.4% of LIS journals are in Portuguese, 13.3% of LIS open access journals are in this language.

These results are consistent with those offered by McVeigh (2004) who gives some data on the regional distribution of the open access journals indexed in the ISI citation databases. According to her "over 40% of the titles from Central or South America are OA journals. In contrast, OA journals from North American and Western Europe comprise 1.5% and 1.1%, respectively, of the total coverage from those regions. For many journals, providing free content online expands their access to an international readership."

Table 1. Number of LIS journals by language.

	LIS journals (Ulrich's)	%	LIS open access journals (DOAJ)	%
Arabic	15	0,4	1	1,3
Bulgarian	6	0,2	1	1,3
Catalan	5	0,1	2	2,7
Chinese	58	1,5	1	1,3
Croatian	8	0,2	1	1,3
Danish	43	1,1	1	1,3
English	2,912	77,5	59	78,7
French	224	6,0	6	8,0
German	212	5,6	4	5,3
Italian	55	1,5	2	2,7
Lithuanian	6	0,2	1	1,3
Norwegian	10	0,3	1	1,3
Polish	26	0,7	1	1,3
Portuguese	53	1,4	10	13,3
Spanish	207	5,5	14	18,7
Swedish	38	1,0	2	2,7
Turkish	2	0,1	1	1,3
Total	3,759	100,0	75	100,0

Ulrich's Periodicals Directory gives us the country of publication of the 59 open access journals included both in DOAJ and Ulrich's Periodicals Directory.

Table 2. Number of LIS open access journals by country of publication

Country	Journals	%
United States	17	28,8
Brazil	7	11,9
United Kingdom	7	11,9
Canada	4	6,8
Spain	4	6,8
Germany	3	5,1
Puerto Rico	2	3,4
15 countries with one journal	15	25,4

Publishers

Most LIS open access journals are published by universities (27 journals, 36.0%) and by professionals associations and societies (18 journals, 24.0%).

Start Year

Just one of the 75 journals included in DOAJ started being published before 1990. This is the case of the *Bulletin des Bibliothèques de France*, published in paper since 1985 and become open access later. Since 1990 the number of open access journals has constantly increased: nine journals were started between 1991 and 1995, 27 between 1996 and 2000, and 27 more between 2000 and 2004. Eleven journals have been started during the last two years so it seems that there is still place for the creation of new LIS open access journals in the near future.

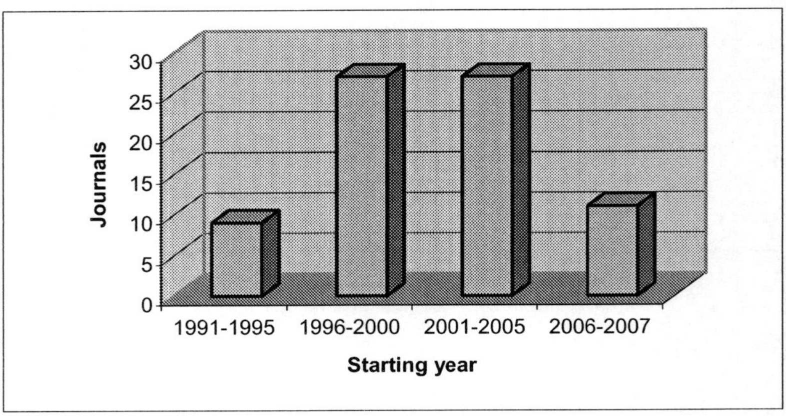

Figure 2. Number of LIS open access journals by starting year.

Frequency

According to Ulrich's Periodicals Directory, open access journals in LIS have a low publication frequency as it is the case for most journals in the field: ten journals (16.9%) are annual, 18 journals (30.5%) are published semi-annually, six journals (10.2%) are published three times a year and 13 journals (22.0%) are published quarterly. Additionally seven journals (11.9%) are published on an irregular basis.

Coverage by Major Abstracting and Indexing Services

The coverage of each of the journals by three major abstracting and indexing services in the field—Library and Information Science Abstracts (LISA), Library, Information Science & Technology Abstracts (LISTA) and Library Literature and Information Science Full Text (LibLit)—was determined[1].

Nearly half of LIS open access journals (34 journals, 45.3%) are present in at least one of the databases: 16 journals (21.3%) are present in all three abstracting and indexing services, 12 journals (16.0%) are abstracted and indexed by two services and 6 journals (8.0%) are present in one database.

The abstracting and indexing service with a major coverage of open access journals is LISTA that indexes 30 (40.0%) of the open access journals included in DOAJ. LISA indexes 24 journals (32.0%) and LibLit indexes 18 journals (24.0%).

At present, three LIS open access journals – *Information Research* and *Journal of the Medical Library Association*– are indexed in the Social Science Citation Index, and one more journal –*Journal of Medical Internet Research*– is indexed in the Science Citation Index.

Characteristics of Digital Open Access Repositories in LIS

Language

The overwhelming majority of the 48 open access digital repositories listed in OpenDOAR (41 repositories, 85.4%) include contents in English. Just four repositories have contents in French and four more include contents in German. Spanish is represented in three repositories, Dutch, Finnish, Italian and Portuguese in two repositories and one single repository includes contents in Hindi and Kannada.

As expected, most of the repositories are based in English-speaking countries: ten repositories are in the United States and eight are in the United Kingdom. Australia, Canada, Germany and India have three repositories, Brazil, Czech

---

1 The list of journals indexed by each database was obtained from:
LISA: http://www.csa.com/factsheets/supplements/lisa.php.
LISTA: http://www.epnet.com/titleLists/lx-coverage.htm.
LibLit: http://vnweb.hwwilsonweb.com/hww/Journals/.

Republic, Italy, Netherlands and Finland have two repositories, and Mexico, Namibia, Norway and South Africa have one single repository with LIS contents each.

These results show some disagreements between the language distribution of open access journals and digital repositories. English is the most usual language in both kind of resources but, although a significant rate of open access journals are published in Spanish and Portuguese, the presence of these languages in digital repositories is marginal.

Software

Most of the repositories listed in OpenDOAR are run either on DSpace (14 repositories, 29.2%) or on EPrints (14 repositories, 29.2%). Both DSpace (http://www.dspace.org) and EPrints (http://www.eprints.org) are open source software for building repositories.

Additionally, three repositories are in HTML, two run on OPUS — both are German — and two run on Wildfire — both based in the Netherlands. Other programs being used are Bepress, HAL, MyCoRe, OAICat and Sunsite.

Size

Forty-four of the repositories listed in OpenDOAR included its size in terms of number of documents included. As shown in Table 3, nearly half of them (20 repositories, 45.5%) have less than 100 documents.

Table 3. Size of open access digital repositories with LIS contents

Size	Repositories	%
< 100 documents	20	45.5
100 – 1,000 documents	14	31.8
> 1,000 documents	10	22.7

Contents

Most of the repositories are institutional and have been created by universities in order to offer its staff a place to store its bibliographic production. Fourteen of the repositories (29.2%) are specialised in LIS while the remaining 34 (70.8%) are multidisciplinary in nature.

Table 4. Contents of LIS open access digital repositories

Contents	Repositories	%
Books	14	29.2
Conferences	30	62.5
Datasets	4	8.3
Learning Objects	5	10.4
Multimedia	7	14.6
Patents	1	2.1
Postprints	14	29.2
Preprints	7	14.6
Publications	22	45.8
References	8	16.7
Special	7	14.6
Theses	23	47.9
Unpublished	27	56.3

When analysing the contents stored in these repositories, we observe that there is a wide diversity of materials. Most of the repositories include conference proceedings (30 repositories, 62.5%), unpublished works (27 repositories, 56.3%), theses (23 repositories, 47.9%) and publications (22 repositories, 45.8%) as shown in Table 4.

CONCLUSIONS

Our results show a dramatic increase in the number of scholarly journals and digital repositories with LIS content freely available through the Internet during the last few years. DOAJ lists 78 open access LIS journals while OpenDOAR lists 48 open access digital repositories with LIS content.

Most LIS open access journals publish articles in English, while a significant rate includes contents in Spanish and Portuguese. However in the case of digital repositories the presence of Spanish and Portuguese is marginal. Almost all LIS open access journals have been created since 1990 at a rate of around 25 journals every five years. It is expected that these figures will continue to increase.

Nearly half of LIS open access journals are present in at least one of the three main abstracting and indexing databases in the field and one fifth of the journals are present in all three databases.

Most open access digital repositories in LIS run either on DSpace or on EPrints. They are mainly university institutional repositories that include a wide diversity of materials, especially conference proceedings, unpublished works, theses and publications.

REFERENCES

Craig, I. D.; Plume, A. M.; McVeigh, M. E.; Pringle, J.; Amin, M. (2007). Do open access articles have greater citation impact? *Journal of Informetrics 1* (3), 239-248.

Fosmire, M.; Young, E. (2000). Free scholarly electronic journals: what access do college and University libraries provide? *College & Research Libraries 61* (6), 500-508.

Hawkings, D. T. (2001). Bibliometrics of electronic journals in information science. *Information Research 7* (1), http://informationr.net/ir/7-1/paper120.html.

Jacsó, P. (2001). Electronic shoes for the cobbler's children: treatment of digital journals in library and information databases. *Online 25* (4), 46-52.

McVeigh, M. (2004). Open Access Journals in the ISI Citation Databases: Analysis of Impact Factors and Citation Patterns.
http://www.thomsonscientific.com/media/presentrep/essayspdf/openaccesscitations2.pdf.

INDEX

D

E

F

G

H

I

N

O

P

Q

R

U

V

W